Every Woman's Guide to

GETTING READY
For the Right Career

By the same Author

Every Woman's Guide to Time Management
Every Woman's Guide to Travel

Every Woman's Guide to

GETTING READY
For the Right Career

Donna Goldfein

Celestial Arts
A Les Femmes Book
Millbrae, California

Celestial Arts
231 Adrian Road
Millbrae, California 94030

First Printing, May, 1981

Cover design by Colleen Forbes
Cover photograph by Martha Brigham

Made in the United States of America

Library of Congress Cataloging in Publication Data

Goldfein, Donna, 1933–
    Getting ready for the right career.

    Bibliography: p.
    1. Vocational guidance for women.   I. Title.
HF5381.G569   650.1'4'024042   80-83692
ISBN 0-89087-935-4 (pbk.)

Contents

Every Woman's Guide to

GETTING READY
For the Right Career

Introduction

Success is often not based on the things one does, as much as the things one does not do.

Not long ago, I heard a respected motivational speaker tell a large audience that single statement had proven more valuable to his success in personal and professional life than any rule he had ever followed. One must develop a keen sense of choice in the daily decisions required for the most effective use of one's time. Those of you who have read my writings on the subject of time management, or have heard me speak, know the respect I have for the precious resource of time.

I have seen countless numbers of people come to my classes and seminars whose complicated and fragmented lifestyles had literally whipped them into a frenzy of confusion and even crisis. Perhaps you feel your life is now galloping by and the reins have slipped from your hands.

You may be one of the numbers a recent survey reported by *Newsweek* magazine. To quote their findings, "No one toils harder at living two lives than the 4.8 million married working mothers of children under six, the fastest-growing segment of the work force. Overall, 43 percent of married mothers with children under six now work outside their homes." Many work out of need rather than choice. "Although Congress has discussed day care endlessly—between 15 and 20 bills relating to the subject have been introduced in every session since 1970—only a few significant measures have passed. . . ." The article concluded with this fact: "Rep. Cardiss Collins (D. Ill.) has been cautiously trying to assemble a package of bills that would include some form of federal funding as well as tax incentives for corporations to subsidize child care . . . administration officials are wary of any comprehensive legislation because of its potentially prohibitive cost—and even day care stalwarts admit glumly that a national system may be a decade away."

It is difficult and many times simply impossible to juggle the responsibilities of home, family and job. Yet millions of American women are trapped in this superwoman squeeze. How has it happened? And, is there a way out? Inflation has contributed to the necessity of the two-paycheck marriage. It is difficult to shift downward after the lifestyle has escalated upward. Additionally, the media are focused upon the self-fulfillment of the career women. However, in reality, isolated millions are struggling with too many responsibilities and too few hours. Little is heard about their needs and wants, and especially their frustrations.

I have written this guide to encourage you to pick up those reins that may have slipped from your hands. I hope you will get a strong grip on them as you read this book. You will feel the support and understanding of others who have shared their experiences of change and growth and who have given me permission to include their stories. Although I have cited some valuable information about the current problems of the working mother and the lack of child care facilities, the thesis of this work is focused upon anyone who is caring for a home, children and sometimes a husband. Many of the women I spoke with were single parents raising their youngsters alone.

When a woman does not work outside the home her status is not clearly defined. She is easy prey for those who consider her always available. Neighbors ask favors regarding child care before or after school. For example, they leave early for work and ask their neighbors who are at home to watch their child for a few minutes if they are delayed getting home, to take packages, to sign for mail, and similar requests. Women confessed they wanted to keep harmony because they did live near one another; however, a number of them were eager to find work to avoid such exploitation. In brief, women often spoke of wanting to escape the stereotype that seemed associated with the woman who remained at home.

Getting Ready is written for you. I believe in you, and the advancement of your personal and professional growth is my objective. In my book, *Every Woman's Guide to Time Management,* I shared with women a back-to-basics, step-by-step program of using time more effectively and managing their homes more efficiently. The ultimate goal was for the homemaker to realize more time for herself.

There was a chapter entitled "Half-Steps" in that book. Half-steps are a way of directing your life to where *you* want to be through the disciplined use of time. Half-steps program a comfortable rhythm of pacing each day by clearly understanding what you want to accomplish and putting aside the things that drain your energy and enthusiasm. You will find half-steps are fifty percent easier than full steps and will direct you toward a chosen destination.

You will enjoy the shared journey as you learn the necessary skills essential for personal and professional growth. I'll introduce you to the strength and support that can be yours through the reading and living of positive thoughts with emphasis on the awareness of how unique and very special you really are. Developing the inner self is a lifetime pursuit. Seeking ways to improve the outer self through physical appearance is an important half-step that promises full step confidence. The essential ingredient necessary to achieve the comfortable rhythm that makes each day a calm serenity is that of order. More space for growth is allowed when one simplifies her surroundings and clarifies her priorities. The guideline is the chapter titled: "Simplify - Satisfy". By simplifying your lifestyle you can satisfy yourself. Once you have completed the homework and cleared the space necessary to move forward, I will introduce an organizational tool to help motivate you toward the goals you have set. Creating the right atmosphere to want to change is essential to *feeling motivated.* Slowly and with continual awareness of the importance of contacts and opportunities, a plan of action develops. The homework you have completed while reading this book will serve you well on the day you choose, or perhaps find it necessary, to enter the competitive job market.

The 3-S notebook will be a ready reference of valuable contacts; the color-coded index card system will have become a working habit; the A.B.E. chart will have provided you with a professional resume; and the taped interviews will have prepared you for the live interview. You will be sensitized to the two V's, the most important assets you can possess in the search for an ideal career. They determine the success of the individual eager for a fulfilling and responsible position and an opportunity to utilize the best of one's skills. The precious days you choose to stay at home can be an investment of great worth and promise big dividends if you practice the half-step program.

Congratulations . . . Now, come along and we will explore this together.

A Very Special
Person . . . You!

I want to share with you a personal experience that caused me to recognize the importance of another person's individual sense of priorities. Respecting the way in which a son or daughter chooses to lead his or her life can be a difficult exercise for parents. The following incident will show you what I mean and explain the effect a poignant comment had upon me.

My eldest daughter and I had just returned from Sunday church service and she was in the living room reading the comics. The coming week was stretched to bursting with many deadlines. Choosing my words carefully, I suggested that it might be a good idea to get a start on the science project due Friday.

Without missing a beat, she looked up at me and said, "Mommie, if God wanted *everything* done today, He wouldn't make tomorrow."

In that instant I had a clear glimpse of the unique individual that she is and realized how important it is to respect the time values of others. We all hear different drummers and listening to the beat that is strong and clear gives us our individuality. My childhood was filled with messages, clearly etched in my memory, from my rural, midwestern background.

My daughter's one statement caused me to question my personal drive to have everything done yesterday. It also made me aware of the uniqueness of the moment which has become a guiding light.

A full awareness of the present is a skill that can be practiced and, with continual use, provide enormous satisfaction. As is true with all new skills, success will depend upon practice and repetition. I'll remind you of this, and as you develop the awareness habit the opportunities for growth will become plentiful. Support will be given by those around you and change will occur without fear.

Take a few moments now to sit very quietly and allow yourself to absorb the beauty of something near you. Perhaps a single tree outside your window has a grace and fragile quality of its limbs that you have never noticed until just now. A moment of awareness has occurred and it is beautiful.

Soon, perhaps your child will walk into the room. Again I encourage you to live the moment. What are you feeling as you see the youngster from this perspective versus the usual pattern of maybe admonishing the child for something unfinished or neglected? The very real unfinished and neglected chores must be put into proper sequence. When a parent practices regular awareness toward a child, their appreciation is sensed and the verbal battle of work delegation is removed. Love flows from the parent toward the child and cooperation results in a mutual respect and understanding. In this atmosphere, a family grows together and not apart.

Children must have love as well as care in order to feel secure and to develop a social self. Speaking of the basic need all of us have for love, I am reminded of an article about the remarkable Dr. Norman Vincent Peale. He had been asked to speak to a group of ministers about what he thought to be most important in the ministers' responsibility to their congregations. He summed up his talk by saying, "Go back to your churches and love your people. That's what it's all about."

Dr. Peale expresses his thoughts so everyone immediately realizes that he has touched directly upon the innermost core. I have been a long-time subscriber to Dr. Peale's inspirational reading. *Guideposts* is an excellent magazine. Pick up a copy and feel the emotions stirred as you learn about countless human experiences. A convenient pamphlet is put out by the Foundation for Christian Living. The title speaks clearly about the contents, *Creative Help for Daily Living*. I had the good fortune to hear Dr. Peale in person a few weeks ago and the memory is still as vivid this moment. The message he shared with a group of national speakers in New Orleans was humorous, poignant, and overflowing with inspiration and enthusiasm. One of the subjects he emphasized was his firm belief in imaging. Allowing the mind to envision something is the first step toward its achievement. Dr. Peale shared countless examples of how imaging had pulled people from despair to hope. He described moving experiences of people who became enormously successful by practicing the acts of imaging. Starting this very minute, give it a chance to work in your life. Think about something you would like to achieve, some goal you have had on a mental To Do List for some time; for example: See yourself signing a contract for your first book. Place this image in front of you each morning and as you continue to work toward your goal, think of the positive and continue to see the image reappear.

Or perhaps you are working toward a degree and juggling responsibilities of home and school. The evening classes seem to have no end. Keep the image alive of seeing yourself reach for the diploma and imagine the feeling you are going to enjoy. O.K., now it's your turn . . . choose your own wish and concentrate. The positive thoughts will reinforce your belief in yourself and invalidate the negative. Create a huge wave of positive feelings in your subconscious and anytime you find your thoughts are causing you to doubt your ability, focus upon the huge wave and literally see the rush of water take away the negative and restore your thinking to the calm and assured poise you desire.

In my book, *Every Woman's Guide to Time Management,* I encourage you to spend time each day enjoying the childlike pleasure of daydreaming. You will be astonished at the experience of peace this gives you. It will tell you many things that you may have never known about yourself. Every day, close your eyes and drift into the fantasy land of daydreaming . . . visualize what you will be in the next phase of your life. As women, we have distinct phases and wherever you are at this time, the normal thrust in daydreaming is to project forward into where you see yourself. If the youngsters are preschool, you may wish they were older and in school. Moving along past school, the thought of their higher education brings with it the need for additional income and possibly the need for you to consider work outside the home. This has become a reality for many and it may be so for you. The chapters here provide a step-by-step program to prepare you for such a change in your lifestyle. Many daydreams have turned into a new awareness of the many opportunities available. Thomas Carlyle spoke with great wisdom when he said, "Silence is the element in which great things fashion themselves." You are a very special person who needs privacy and quiet after a day filled with noise, interruptions and demands. Take that time, read something to create a mood of positive thinking, and practice the art of imaging. You will find this time a daily award you give to yourself and it will serve as an energizer to refresh you physically and spiritually.

As you think so shall you be. Allow fresh, new creative thoughts to flow into your mind. It was the great philosopher William James who observed, "The greatest discovery of my generation is that human beings can alter their lives by altering their attitudes."

An obscure novelist named Walter Gerhardie commented, "In every situation one of two things happens: either the situation changes or our attitude toward it changes. No feeling, no situation lasts forever."

Let's look at the situation in your life at this moment and take an inventory of all your treasures. This is not going to be a list of material possessions because they provide surface pleasure. You possess hidden assets that can make your life an exciting journey. Too often we take our precious senses for granted. We use our ability to hear and see, to smell, touch and taste constantly. But, do we need to be reminded what the loss of any of our senses would mean to us? Helen Keller, who at the age of two suffered an illness and lost her ability to see, to hear and to speak, represents a challenge to us all. Throughout her life she aided the cause of the handicapped by her worldwide travels, her writing and the example of her indomitable faith and spirit. Her Bible in braille was always near and was worn down from use. She made it a permanent part of her life and received its power. We become blind to the riches we possess and take them for granted. This quote from one of Helen Keller's well-known writings, *Three Days to See*, serves as a visual reminder from one who could not see. I keep it where I can see and read it often; you may want to do the same.

"I who am blind can give one hint to those who see: use your eyes as if tomorrow you would be stricken blind. And the same method can be applied to the other senses. Hear the music of voices, the song of a bird, the mighty strains of an orchestra, as if you would be stricken deaf tomorrow. Touch each object you want to touch as if tomorrow your tactile sense would fail. Smell the perfume of flowers, taste with relish each morsel, as if tomorrow you could never smell and taste again. Make the most of every sense; glory in all the facets of pleasure and beauty."

Earlier this afternoon, I consciously and carefully practiced this woman's wisdom. Walking along the water's edge on my way to the office, I stopped to listen to the lovely Italian music a number of elderly men were enjoying while they watched their contemporaries playing the traditional game of bocce ball. Every afternoon the same crowd gathers and shares the companionship and the competitiveness of this experience. Moving along toward my office, I noticed a number of tourists poring over a city map and I asked if there was something I might help them find. Their surprise and genuine appreciation has stayed in my memory. That kind of experience can soften the moments of the day.

For most of us, it is easier to talk than it is to listen. The ability to listen is a skill that takes practice. Thoreau said, "'Tis better to ask questions than to know all the answers." That makes a lot of sense. Think about asking questions as a part of the listening skill. Everyone we meet is an individual who needs to be heard. Every human being needs to know that someone genuinely cares what he or she is saying.

My purpose is to demonstrate the reasons you will

want to perfect your listening and awareness skills. Your personal and professional growth will soar in direct relationship to the increased audience you solicit. That audience should include neighbors, friends, store owners, newspaper reporters, church organizations and parent groups. As you clarify your professional goals you will probably become involved in continuing education, special skills courses, professional organizations and counseling.

This is not too early to introduce a very important item—a contact book—in the form of a simple, small, spiral notebook. Fondly referred to as the 3-S contact book, it is exactly as I described: simple, small and spiral . . . a bound notebook in a size you find appropriate and convenient to carry with you all of the time.

The purpose of the 3-S contact book is to collect contacts; to confirm and nurture those contacts until the time comes when you are ready to ask advice and assistance of those friends. They will have become your friends because you will have practiced the first rules of making friends while exploring potential employment directions.

Dale Carnegie wrote a set of simple and practical steps to follow. His book, *How to Make Friends and Influence People,* has provided guidance for millions of readers. Many others have tried to say the same thing but miss the point because the meaning gets lost in the convoluted verbiage of buzz words or complex analysis. His six rules are basic. Put them to work in your life. They are dynamite.

1. Become genuinely interested in others.

2. Smile.

3. Remember the person's name.

4. Be a good listener.

5. Ask about the interests of the other person.

6. Make others feel important and do it sincerely.

Studies have shown that people are controlled by early conditioning and that ninety percent of what we do is out of habit. Because you may not have thought about active listening before, it may be easier if I suggest a small personal goal. Today: Listen intently to the next three people you talk with and try to put yourself in their place for a moment. Concentrate on the words your hear them speaking and show concern and care about what they are saying. Smile, if that is appropriate. In any event, let them see your acceptance of them and let them know how you feel. I am not suggesting that you attempt to correct or resolve the problems that they may share with you. It is the act of listening that will help them to help themselves. Creative, constructive listening involves opening your mind to hear and understand what is going on inside another person. While you are intently listening to someone, that person feels loved and accepted. People thrive on friendship. It makes people happy to be with people who care about them and love them. Regardless of whether it is a stranger or a member of one's own family, a good listener cares.

The ability to really listen takes practice and this is why you must make a daily commitment to start with just three people every day. As the habit becomes familiar, the warmth you experience will propel you on toward the practice of listening creatively all the time. This is an apprenticeship toward the time when listening will make contacts which will create business opportunities. Case histories of successful business people are often filled with accounts of how initial contacts grew to become a large payroll of employees. Often the subject is an enterprising human with the ability to listen.

I want to help you understand how the art of communicating can be practiced. You possess a very special ability to listen creatively and here is a simple and sure way to become aware of those people you meet daily.

Purchase a small spiral notebook and use this book each day to jot down personal observations and thoughts you have about any three people you meet that day. Because this is a new exercise, let me give you a personal example of how a typical day looks in my first notebook entry.

Monday, early a.m. Gregg. Shell station. 25th and Calif. The explanation of this message is complex; however, I want to share all the details so you fully understand my urging you to use this system.

I had stopped for gasoline at 6:30 a.m. and commented to the attendant about the early hour and asked if he was a student. From this single question I learned that he worked two hours before school and four hours in the evening. He helped to support his mother and a younger brother because his father had been killed. His interest was in electronics and he wanted to find weekend work that would assure his having a full-time summer job.

I took Gregg's name and number and told him I would let him know if I heard anything. The next day I took our table model T.V. to a neighborhood television repair. Practicing the art of listening creatively, I started a conversation with the owner of the shop. I mentioned the ambitious high school senior working down the street at the Shell station. The shop owner was so impressed with Gregg's background that he asked if I would have him stop by and talk about weekend work. A few words of conversation and a sincere caring about other people will add an extra special moment to an ordinary day. The elation and excitement on Gregg's face when I told him the news made my day.

Gregg is now training in a special electronics class, working weekends at the television repair and has a full-time job for the summer.

Second entry that day.

Savings and Loan District Manager. I jotted his name and phone number directly into my spiral notebook from the business card he handed me. Cards are easily lost and follow-up on contacts prove easier when they are accessible in one place—the 3-S notebook. Explanation: I had stopped by to ask the manager some questions my class had raised about investments. I was also planning a series of seminars and wanted to have a representative of a savings and loan on the panel to share first-hand information. This contact resulted in booking my time management workshops into a number of their branch offices. Contacts do result in contracts.

Third entry that same day was a single word.

I had entered *Family.* This was to remind myself to be extra sensitive to my family's messages to me. Take the time to see and to hear. How often we simply nod and agree when someone speaks. If your child is talking to you, a few minutes of intense listening is worth an hour of nods and partial attention. We all become victims of habit and putting reminders on paper helps. Making the single statement—*Family*—provides a visual reminder that I should practice active listening at all times. It takes only a few moments to write your feelings in this notebook and I urge you to start the habit today. Doing so will pull you into the practice of seeing and hearing those around you.

Not long ago, a young mother was telling me how she felt about working outside the home. She confessed she thought society was at the office. Once she decided her youngster was her first priority and that she would stay at home during his early years, the truth of the situation came to her. Society is everywhere. She found enormous social interaction in listening to the neighborhood grocer and the widow down the street and the postman and the milkman. The joy she felt came from releasing her dormant resource of sensitivity for all people. Her caring developed into great sharing and the contacts she nurtured provided help in many ways.

Society has programmed many to believe women must work outside the home in order to achieve feelings of self-worth and accomplishment. If staying at home with her family is to be an option for a woman, it is essential that support be given to this decision. My contribution toward this support is to share the program of personal time management that is working for many homemakers. The reader of my *Every Woman's Guide to Time Management* will remember my message includes a system of organization, planning and doing. However, the key to any fulfilling lifestyle is the forming and maintaining of close human relationships. That is the essence and the core of what life is really all about, and without it not anything one does means a great deal.

Northwestern sociologist Norman Bradburn conducted a study about happiness and gave a long list of questions to the people he interviewed. The results indicated people were happy when they accomplished something or been complimented. The interesting fact was this: The best predicator of happiness was the number of contacts with people and it did not seem to matter how those contacts were made. Happy people just had more get-togethers with friends and more outings and meals away from home and contacts with people in general. Barbra Streisand has brought an important message about caring to us in her well-received hit record, in which she sings the words "people who need people are the luckiest people in the world."

It has been said that people live in a very restricted social circle compared to their potential. Just how small is your circle and are you ready to change the size of the arena in which you live? The assignments I suggest at the end of each chapter are planned in a chronological journey. Following along in sequence will assure you of reaching your destination. Along the way you will have demonstrated your determination and proven to yourself the ability to take action toward making changes now will be invaluable to your personal and professional growth.

Assignments

1. Practice the awareness habit—it pays big dividends.

2. Read inspirational literature; it will turn your thinking into the *winner's way of life.*

3. Dream about what you think you want to do. Visualize yourself reaching for the goal you seek.

4. Purchase a 3-S contact book—the simple, small, spiral notebook to carry with you and write impressions, thoughts, goals and dreams. The purpose of the book is to collect contacts that will provide ideas and introductions for you at the time you need them.

5. Listen intently to three people each day. Concentrated listening is a skill that when fully developed can benefit you in your personal and professional life. Enlarge your circle of friends and acquaintances. The result will be beneficial to your future goals.

Personal Growth Experience

"I find the great thing in this world is not so much where we stand as in what direction we are moving."

Oliver Wendell Holmes

The direction in which you are moving is forward. If you have reached this point, your awareness is keen and your attitude ready for change. Getting ready for the career you want to have someday will mean seeking the counsel of experts, risking the disapproval of some friends, and growing in a way that is wonderful.

Are you ready for change? Would you like to start with your personal appearance? Why not! The marvelous support the outer self will give to the inner self is worth an investment of time and money to you. The question asked by many who are ready for a new look and eager to seek help is simply, "Where do I start?"

15

According to my close friend and president of Successful Images, Diane Parente, women seek her guidance because they want expert advice. Diane compared their engaging her to the way they would call an interior decorator to help avoid costly errors in home furnishings. The time and expense invested in clothing errors heap a load of guilt upon women and fill closets with mistakes. When I asked Diane why more women did not seek personal help in making their clothing selections, she said, "The fear of change keeps them from asking for professional assistance. They feel safe with the image they have grown accustomed to accept as *their look*." The style, colors, textures, and accessories change with the season and for those intent on wearing a type of uniform, the effect can often look dated. No one will deny it may be comfortable. Old habits are always the most comfortable and the most difficult to change. Wearing the same type of clothing and neglecting to change with the times is an indication that you are stuck with old habits and the result is unattractive.

Not long ago I spoke with Kathleen, an attractive woman in her late forties. She was beautifully dressed in a conservative beige suit that complimented her coloring and a lovely pale green blouse. It was not coincidence that the shade of green in her blouse was identical to the color of her eyes. It had been planned and so had every item Kathleen was wearing. I share this personal story of Kathleen because it supports the change that came about in her life when she paid for guidance in creating the image she needed. Kathleen had worked for the same company ever since she graduated from college, had not married, was unhappy both about her position with the firm and for waiting too many years to take action to change. Her inner self was telling her a message about assertiveness and all her prepared speeches and attempts to speak with her superiors collapsed before they were ever uttered. Kathleen was the victim of her outer self and the way she looked.

As Ms. Parente describes it, "Clothing makes a personal statement about oneself. This image is the first impression the public has upon which to make decisions."

The impression is critical at the time of job interviews. Equally as critical is the impression you make upon any person with whom you wish to build confidence and respect of your ability.

With this in mind, the help Kathleen sought resulted in her gaining a strong professional image and self-confidence. These two assets provided her with courage to change jobs and she now considers her new position a career.

Richard Lathrop defines a career in his excellent guide, *Who's Hiring Who,* as "employment that uses all of your abilities, experience and potential for growth and that will produce the best long-term results for you."

Not everyone will want to invest the money or admit they need the help of professional clothing experts. Through my research and interviews on the pros and cons of this service, I have come to agree with those who are working in the field of *image making.* The experts feel that when a woman is willing to pay for professional consultation she has achieved an attitude of wanting to change. She seeks the direction of someone who she believes knows what to suggest and select that will create the best look. Additionally, the woman may want to create a new image to fit a change in lifestyle or a new career, or simply to shop for a travel wardrobe that will pack well. The reasons may vary slightly; however, the underlying cause is a wish to make the very best of her looks by complimenting her appearance with the perfect choice of clothing.

That may sound like a great deal to expect; however, the chances of success are much more in one's favor if someone thoroughly alert to the current fashion picture and knows the merchandise in the store, and perhaps many stores, can preselect garments to help you in the decision. The methods used by those in the professional style careers differ. Basically, however, the inventory prepared for the client offers a practical and sensible approach to the situation. Some that I studied included a full account of the lifestyle and personal preferences of the client. Exact measurements of her figure are taken and observations about the body structure and best type of clothing to maximize her assets are noted. An inventory of her current wardrobe and convenient items to fill in at the time shopping become the object. The program is focused upon a thorough understanding of the woman's preferences and her plans for the future as they pertain to her wardrobe needs. Additionally, an accounting of everything in the wardrobe is an excellent base from which to start culling items that detract from creating that individual look which is so special. The image consultants suggested that coordinating clothing is easier if one selects from a single designer line. That individual has already spent much time blending fabrics, styles and textures to create a fashionable look. Looking carefully at the top designers' styles for the season can be an excellent guide for you to follow.

The question of hemlines kept coming up during seminar discussions in regard to dressing and current style. The consensus seemed to be that there are no hard and fast rules about lengths. The good judgment of the individual who knows best the length that is most flattering to her figure is most appropriate. There is a simple rule for building of a workable closet, filled with a group of "friends" that seem ready and willing to make you feel comfortable, look color-coordinated and show you cared enough to pay the cost necessary for a smashing look.

The four "C's" that I have used in the above sentence will include: Comfort, Color (that flatters), Coordinated items and the Cost merits the investment of something very special.

You may find the guidance of an expert will save you many hours of confusion. Also, the investment may prove worthy because of the errors that you will avoid in the future.

Asking friends and checking listings in the yellow pages are two simple ways of locating the names of those who have good reputations in the field. The listing may be under Image Consultant. Color Analysis is another category that can include the full package of color, clothing and purchasing of the garments. Check with colleges in your area offering continuing education programs. Some of the experts teach courses on the subject. I have been sharing my Time Management and Travel courses in continuing education for many years. Send for local college catalogs and brochures to look over the areas you may find important for self-growth. An excellent selection of subjects is often available.

What should one do about a weight problem if the intention is to diet before clothing consultation?

Answer: Diet first and then invest the time and money.

I asked one of the consultants this question and her answer was candid. "I have a policy that every client must arrange for a free half-hour consultation prior to deciding our working together can be mutually beneficial. During that time I approach the subject of weight straight on. If weight is an obvious problem, I ask if she is comfortable with her weight. If the person is a size 16 and has accepted this as the image she can live with and has no desire to change her size, the inner self has made the decision and it is only a manner of dressing the outer self at this point. The selection available in sizes 14 and 16 happen to be far greater than in a size 6. An attractive wardrobe is easily assembled for the larger woman and the look is totally complimentary."

Attitude plays an enormous role where weight is concerned. So much has been said about weight and diets that perhaps you are as dubious as I am about the effectiveness of the thousands upon thousands of diet clinics, spas, classes, workshops, seminars, and the neverending articles, books, and promises.

How about condensing a weight-loss formula into a single sentence? Eat only half as much, chew it twice as long and spend ten full minutes on regular exercise daily. Your self-confidence will zoom upward when you see a reflection in the mirror you like and it is *you.* The image you carry in your mind is often the one your mirror will reflect. Until the mirror reflects an image you are happy with, the ability to carry yourself with poise and assurance is slightly diminished.

The simple formula of half as much food chewed twice as long does not seem to be quite the battle of discipline as is a regular exercise program. Establish a daily habit and not a hit-and-miss routine. I find our energetic and eager house dog, Duchess, is like an alarm clock and our morning runs benefit me as much as they do the pet. However, without Duchess' insistence I know the habit would be much more difficult to do daily.

> *Secret:* Find something or someone to push you to exercise every day and visualize the look *you* want to attain. Put a special pair of slacks or a good-looking new pantsuit where you see it each day, something you want to wear soon but at this time is just not the right size. Many women with whom I spoke confessed they had a couple of distinct clothing sizes, one group for their heavier times and another group of clothes that fit them when they lost some weight. Have you different sizes in the same

closet? Join the crowd and know you have much company. However, the size to strive for and keep is the size that you want to be and think you look the best . . . agree?

The opportunity to use the days when you are not working outside of the home can provide an ideal springboard to new adventures. Especially important in the job market is the ability to communicate effectively. Contacts who are part of your daily life can become subjects for you in exercising one of the essentials of good conversation, finding a topic of interest to the other person. You will find this daily training becomes a good habit. Remember when I suggested the exercise of speaking to three people each day and concentrating on your ability to listen? Do this daily and write down their names and other information of importance in identifying the person, together with your comments in the 3-S notebook. That very special simple, small, spiral book is going to provide you with a list of important contacts at the time you want most to pick up a ready-made source of introductions and support. Not each and every entry will prove useful. As you keep the notebook current, the names you collect will become more meaningful. You will begin to see the help they can be in the future and, in turn, you may be of assistance to them in some way. The building of the "network" is the professional term and it is easily done once you get started. Pacing yourself to steadily accomplish a little at a time is the secret toward the control of time and of yourself.

Communications skills can be improved daily. Your family and friends will benefit when you start seriously concentrating on listening. Improving your personal relationships with them is an added bonus.

Communicating is a matter of exchanging thoughts. Studies show that those who communicate well in an interview score very high. Eighty percent of the decision to hire rests upon whether or not the potential employee has the ability to sell herself. To speak and to be understood is an asset that will serve you well in whatever you do.

The training I was given by American Airlines to prepare me for a career as a stewardess included a wealth of communication clues that I will capsulize and share with you. The term "stewardess" is a clue which indicates that the era of my flight days preceded the current "flight attendant" title. Following college, I knew I did not want to follow my major but satisfied my restlessness through my choice of an airline career. Our training was held in very cramped quarters at Midway Airport in Chicago. The intensity of that experience and the information we absorbed during those few weeks imbued us with communication skills that will last a lifetime. Not any number of books, tapes, months of instruction, or private counseling could have proven as effective as the concentrated course our well-trained instructors delivered. As eager trainees, our attitude was equally primed to receive the information and thus we had the ideal conditions for learning.

Enormous amounts of information had to be memorized on every phase of our responsibility from meal service to emergency procedures. Because each young woman was fully concentrating and intensely eager to pass the rigorous course to win her silver wings, the lessons were learned.

A remarkable woman served as the supervisor of the instructors, and her appearance, poise, and ability to articulate with enthusiasm, wit, and strength provided a role model for us all. She spoke to the class on our first day of training. Her message lives with me today. She said:

"Each of you have just been given a unique and rare

opportunity. Only one out of every hundred applicants is selected to join our ranks and to have this honor is special. I congratulate each of you and look forward to personally knowing you during the weeks to follow. This is the first day of an intense schedule of very demanding study. Some of you may not make it through the test and for that I am sorry. For those of you who are willing to put everything you have into hours and hours of study, testing, trying, doing, and sometimes even crying, your efforts will be well rewarded."

This dynamic woman went on to explain the urgent need for more stewardesses to cover the holiday traffic and advanced our date of graduation to December 24. That shortened the training period by a full week, so incredible effort was required of every student.

Not everyone did survive the pressure and the tight schedule; however, those who did were exceptional stewardesses. The opportunity to help the airline at a crucial time was uppermost in our minds and it worked like magic. We felt a common bond by having come through a special crises together. At the beginning of our first week of training, the supervisor again came into our classroom and asked for a few moments to share some valuable words about our primary duty to our passengers. She introduced to us the art of communicating that each of you can apply and practice daily. You will soon see remarkable results. This was her message:

"The airplane is your living room and the passengers are invited guests who have dropped by to see you. The warmth and hospitality you would extend to personal friends coming by your home is the kind of reception you will give the person boarding that plane. Within moments the individual will not be a stranger and all because of how you communicate. Never fail to give everyone stepping onto the airplane an immediate warm welcome. And listen carefully now, I want you to look directly into the eyes of everyone who steps into that cabin. A brief eye-to-eye contact will establish a hospitable atmosphere faster than hours of meal service or giving out pillows. Let the individual know how pleased you are to have him or her on the flight and that you really care. Shortly after takeoff you will be taking the passengers' names. This is the opportunity to repeat their names, concentrate on memorizing as many as you can, and say something personal that will flatter or compliment, or in some way put a bright touch to their day. When time from your procedures allows, become a good listener. One last word about the mood you transmit to the passengers sitting in your cabin. As you start the trip, before anyone boards the plane, mentally unload your personal worries and cares. Place them in an imaginary suitcase and drop that case outside the plane. The inner feeling you will experience, following a trip, that you have left your worries behind and cared about your passengers and their concerns . . . that feeling will be one of satisfaction. You will know you have done your very best. My congratulations to each of you."

That happened many years ago. The lesson was one we adopted into our lives and used in both our professional and personal daily contacts with people. Her message was a quest for excellence. Too many times we cheat ourselves by accepting less than best. When we do our best, we feel personal recognition and it makes us feel very much alive.

There is a true story about employees in a paper bag factory that will give another example of how personal pride makes a difference. This appeared in the Christopher pamphlet, *What A Day This Can Be,* by John Catoir.

"When the St. Regis Paper Company's plant in

Vernon, California had a quality control problem, employees were asked how to cut the reject rate. They suggested that making each worker responsible for his or her production would do the trick. Each bag now bears the maker's initials. Productivity is higher and employee morale is up. The plant's rejection rate is less than half of one percent, and workers agree that personal pride made the difference."

People have a human longing to make their lives meaningful and rich. Not always rich in material success but rather in the human core through developing relationships that give them the feeling of love. The sense of personal pride you take in doing whatever job for which you may be responsible at this time can produce startling results.

Much of the emphasis on communication is placed upon the technique of verbally communicating the words. Classes on the methods and means of communication are taught daily. However, they are teaching the theory only which does not guarantee that people will learn to communicate. The skill will be mastered only if it is practiced immediately. Knowledge that is used will stick in your mind and unless it is used within the first twenty-four hours of having heard it, the chances of loss are great. Incorporate what it is you want to use and do so quickly. The time, persistence, and daily application may not be easy. I hope you give the following assignment a try for two full weeks and see if you notice the results.

Assignment

1. Wardrobe update: Specify the date you want to complete the full clearing and condensing of your wardrobe.

2. Decide whether or not to seek professional help.

3. If you are assembling your own "total look", allow yourself sufficient time to be selective. Give much thought to the 4 C's of the wardrobe: Comfort, Color, Coordination, Cost.

4. Weight loss program:
    Eat half the amount
    Chew twice as long
    Exercise ten minutes daily

5. Communication is a skill that improves through use. Practice
    a. Listening intently
    b. Establishing eye-to-eye contact
    c. Showing sincere interest and concern for the other person.

6. Seek the best. Your quest for excellence will achieve admirable results.

Simplify - Satisfy

Simplify your lifestyle—Satisfy yourself.

Does that sound appealing? Does just hearing the word "simplify" seem to release pressure and offer some freedom from stress? Life has become complex because too many things are happening at the same time. The result is too much clutter—and clutter breeds confusion. Over and over again the problems of today's lifestyles are discussed and complicated systems developed to teach us to cope. The best way to solve any problem is to clearly define it, locate the source of the trouble, and work logically toward permanent solutions. This may sound like an over-simplification but it cuts through the confusion and gives us some answers.

Simplify means to reduce the excess and this requires decisions. The individual decisions will not always seem important; however, ultimately they will be crucial to the removal of the clutter that develops. Our homes, apartments, flats, and studios are continually deluged with letters, papers, circulars, invitations, notices, advertisements, samples, catalogs, books, and bills. What do you do with the paper flow? Start making decisions to protect hours which can be better spent getting ready for the future and human relationships. First, it is essential to become aware of the time it takes to sort through all of the paper. The culprit word used in that sentence is "sort." Think of the times you have moved one stack of bills and under it uncovered another stack of correspondence while attempting to find something else you need. Then a phone call will distract you and you must start all over again sorting through the clutter.

Any of my students of personal time management may pass over this and move along to the next chapter. My book, *Every Woman's Guide to Time Management,* is a detailed guide to managing a household more effectively in order to have personal time to enjoy. The success of the program depends on one's ability to change the poor habits that bog one down in daily routine and introduce more effective ways of using the time given equally to everyone. Control of one's hours requires decisions on how time can best be spent in a given circumstance. Removing the clutter and consequently simplifying one's life is equally beneficial to the working woman, working man or the full-time homemaker or husband. For those of you who are not familiar with my time management program, following is a condensed version.

First, the organization of a *think center* will create a positive attitude and make it infinitely easier for you to simplify. This important step forward will happen more easily if you give yourself permission to use an appropriate area in your home for a desk, some portable file boxes, and the basic supplies you need for an organized system of handling the paper and correspondence. Portable file boxes are more efficient that one large, standing metal case because they work with today's need to take the files and go. If you are active on boards, or work with school, community, and church groups, you know the amount of paper generated by each can become excessive. The problem occurs when you are already late and can't find what you need. It takes time to pull the papers you need from a large, standard metal file case and put them into a briefcase or carryall. This is why the convenient, mobile carrying case is a winner.

I have developed a time saving formula that you may want to try. It is the A.F.T. method of alleviating paper clutter and it works on the principle that handling a piece of paper more than once takes twice as much time.

A. Act on every piece of paper you pick up.

F. File only that which is absolutely necessary.

T. Throw away the rest.

Remember: Handle a piece of paper one time only.

If your family includes school-age children, encourage them to prepare their own portable files that will hold the rosters, notices, papers and information that continually flows from their school and other organizations. Following your initial training session on how the file works, you can teach them the A.F.T. method.

Start a file box labeled *Household Information* and use a "fat file" system. The instruction manual, warranty, and any essential papers for all appliances should be kept in one "fat file" under *Appliances.* Another, labeled *Automobiles,* eliminates the frustration of searching for service records and registrations when they are needed. *Taxes* is another "fat file" for deduction verification, information, and important papers necessary for the preparation and filing of your Federal and State income tax returns. When bills come across your desk, they can immediately be dropped into the "fat file" for *Bills.*

When your Household Information file is clearly identified, the responsibility can be shared. Likewise, anyone needing the information can find it easily and without waiting for you. I remember a friend saying about a co-worker, "The trouble with him is that he carries the office around in his head which makes it impossible to know where anything is or to cooperate on mutual projects." When a *think center* is established in the home it will improve cooperation once all members realize how efficiently it works.

Be sure to stock it well with supplies including everything from paper clips to a wall-type pencil sharpener. Having a good supply of the frequently used items around will simplify your daily routine.

Speaking of daily routine, consider a typical morning in your life and retrace your usual procedure. How are you awakened? Does your body tense up in reaction to a shrill alarm or are you pleasantly coaxed to consciousness by the soothing music of a clock radio? Do you smell coffee brewing and feel eager for that first cup? If you are a coffee lover, invest in an automatic timer that will start your coffee a few minutes before your radio goes off. The tone of the day will be set in pleasure and peace. For the mother of young children, maybe with both an infant and a toddler demanding early morning attention, the first cup of coffee can get the day off to a good start.

One of my close friends and associate in teaching the time management classes is the mother of five young children. She starts each day with a full hour to herself for meditation, a long walk with the dog, and some quiet time which she spends reading. She uses those very early hours for herself. The day gets off to a flying start when the household begins to stir but she needs that hour of privacy to gather inner calmness and to consider her many blessings. The extra hour in the morning is almost everyone's favorite time for sleep, and yet a change in routine can create a new awareness. Awareness plays an important role in one's desire to simplify. Take some time to consider the room you see first thing in the morning. The visual attractiveness of a bedroom and the comfort of your bath will depend on the attention you have given to simplicity. Distraction occurs when you can't find what you want because of clutter. Too many items not having a proper place—that is clutter. Too many books not read, too many magazines stacked up, half-done projects, and boxes of things you plan to get to one day. Does that sound vaguely familiar? Make a decision to clear away all of the things that are not helping you. Clear away items not giving you pleasure or providing inspiration. Surround yourself with only meaningful things: your favorite photos, a single rose in a crystal vase, a firm and comfortable bed, and your favorite chair. Adequate lighting is missing in many homes, particularly in the bedroom. Concentrate on changes that will provide the total relaxation this room must give you.

Let me share the description of a traditional Japanese inn, referred to as the *ryokan,* and reported about by foreign correspondent Bob Dunham. Having spent twenty years in Japan as a freelance writer, his reports are glowing. "Staying at a ryokan represents a total experience . . . a step out of our complicated world of congestion into a dreamworld where the word ryokan itself conjures up a host of pleasing images: relaxation, simplicity, comfort, tranquility, leisure . . . and conscientious care for the tired traveler, exhausted businessman, or even a quiet romance-seeking couple . . . There is nothing else in the world quite like it. A ryokan represents the *ultimate experience in the art of Japanese living, a serene world* of ancient and fortunately well-preserved Japanese culture and customs." This reporter's article was so well written that I found myself wishing it were possible to take off immediately for Japan. But, wait a moment—why not create a private ryokan and enjoy the same simplicity and serenity in our own setting?

In Bob Dunham's article, he speaks of the "uncluttered quality and extreme cleanliness" of the room. I especially enjoyed his confession, "As you sit taking in all this simple, refined beauty, you are almost shocked by the wonderful quietness of the room." Are you motivated to want this type of atmosphere yourself?

The mood he describes has been carefully and purposely created to assure the guest total relaxation. This experience can really be enjoyed in the privacy of your own home. Let me suggest the first steps and you will be motivated to improve and embellish them in your personal style to achieve a private ryokan of your own.

The first step will be to delegate to paper your plans for clearing away the unnecessary items that are taking up valuable space. Often I use the reminder that "clutter breeds confusion" and when the clutter is removed the result is open space. Open space provides a feeling of inner tranquility because the mind is not preoccupied with the clutter which tends to pull and tug at the subconscious. Get the useless things out of your living area. Ask yourself why any part of your home should act as a storage area for items that fail to give you help, support, or pleasure. Articles outgrow their usefulness and must be discarded to clear open space so necessary for simplicity. If the task seems complex and you don't know where to start, consider a project each week. I like to use 3"×5" index cards in a variety of colors for motivation. A detailed explanation of how I use them will follow in the next chapter. For now, however, I only want to encourage you to jot down a list of the projects you wish to complete in your quest to simplify your surroundings and satisfy yourself.

An excellent place to start is your clothes closet, and once this area becomes controlled, the immediate results are noticed daily. Clothing that is taking up space in your closet should be working for you and not mocking you. If you feel less than great about the garments, begin the simplification procedure immediately. Take a couple of large cardboard boxes and place them near the closet. Set a timer for one hour and start this decision-making exercise. Ask yourself, "Will I wear this anymore? Where? When?" And be honest with your answers. In my time management book I refer to the "for sure" items in your wardrobe. Any clothing you reach for when you want to dress quickly and look your best is a "for sure" winner. Then there are those over which you hesitate and say, "Maybe one day I'll need this," or the classic remark about "how much *good* is still left" in the item. Listen to the things you are saying and notice how they tend to sell you on putting the garment right back into the closet where it will add clutter and confusion for another six months or maybe even a year. Give away those items that evoke a "maybe I will" and allow the good in the garment to benefit someone who really needs and will use it.

There will be a few items you may wish to pair up with a new blouse, sweater, or an accessory to update the look. Remove them from your closet to another place until you shop for the companion piece. Take the item along when you go shopping and the result will be more satisfactory.

While you are cleaning out your closet, clear the dresser drawers and any shelves of items that have not been used recently. The project will be completed quickly if the timer is set to create a deadline and you work in a smooth and uninterrupted manner.

Let me pause at this time to talk about the importance of focusing on the message of *Getting Ready*. As you move along, clearing your living space and removing excess things, you will start to feel in control of your time. It is essential to eliminate the time wasters that have drained your energies in order to organize a system which will motivate you to move swiftly through the daily procedures of dressing, grooming, planning, cooking, eating, reading, and writing. A comfortably paced system for personal and professional growth will develop as you follow through on the assignments. For example, at this moment a professional career may be far removed from your thoughts and you may not be anticipating any additional demands upon your time. However, we do not know exactly what tomorrow may bring. Should the need to work become essential in your life, the half-steps that I am introducing to you now of pulling your home and yourself together in readiness for a future time, will serve to provide great confidence and comfort.

As you well know, the immediate everyday needs involving food, clothing, shelter, and personal care of oneself and one's family can take the entire day. Grocery shopping alone can legitimately fill a full morning or afternoon, particularly for the homemaker who may use the diversion to fulfill her need for adult association. A busy mother of small children may find her days filled but without the stimulation of shared conversation on an adult level. Habits develop and years pass and she is still shopping in the manner which may have been appropriate during the early years of child rearing. The outing itself fills a very real need and I can empathize with so many of you who would be delighted to trade in the chore of repetitive grocery shopping. You feel a great need to do something more constructive with those hours. The self-actualization that is repeated in the writings of Abraham Maslov should be your goal.

Until the path is cleared of the routine management chores that capture and keep you their slave, you cannot comfortably move on to another phase of your life. The slavery to which I refer is not involved with people but rather to bad habits and archaic ways of home management.

First, let's take an objective look at your purchasing habits, preparation, and even presentation of food. Do you plan shopping, take full responsibility for buying the food, and prepare it, repeating the same familiar menus? Does all this become monotonous? Change is essential to avoid boredom. Solution: Delegate others to help with shopping for groceries. Smile and praise their efforts, in spite of the wrong brands, different amounts, and even types of food from those on your grocery list. Correction or criticism will result in your taking back the chore and then you will be back at square one. Keep an ongoing grocery list in a prominent spot such as the refrigerator door, bulletin board or inside a front cupboard door. Same place and always rotating is the clue to making the list work. With a menu plan for the week and a well-stocked pantry, once a week shopping, and an occasional stop for dairy and perishable items should do it. Be ready for an assortment of impromptu meals. The storage area should contain supplies you can reach for the moment extra plates must be set for a meal. An initial inventory and stocking of supplies will take advance planning and some monetary outlay; however, an enormous saving in time spent standing in lines at checkout counters makes this effort worthwhile.

Paper products and staples can be purchased in advance and stored. It will simplify your routine if a miniature retail store (storage of kleenex, toilet tissue, shampoo, toothpaste, mouthwash, light bulbs) is available in the area of your kitchen or hall closet. Think of the control you can have over the management of your routine duties when the old habit of buying a single package of light bulbs or one box of kleenex is replaced with the purchase of a year's supply. You become an inventory manager and it is a great deal easier to cope with a low supply than no supply. In a factory when supplies are not available, production ceases. What do you think happens in your life when you reach for the shampoo and find none or when you are borrowing a light bulb from one lamp to use in another? An investment of one shopping excursion for a six- to twelve-month inventory makes good business sense. Managing a home is a business. Many family members may be living in that home and things tend to bog down when supplies are gone.

If you want the convenience enough you will become creative in locating or creating storage space. Under the basement steps is our solution. One afternoon was spent arranging the shelves. A large tablet for inventory of yearly supplies is kept nearby. Supplies are stacked neatly in this out-of-the-way space. Consider adding a shelf above the one almost every hall closet traditionally seems to possess. Why all that wasted space that stretches up to the ceiling? Stack books (about ten work nicely) on either end of the built-in shelf to provide support for a shelf to hold the supplies needed for effective management of the kitchen and bathroom.

A neighbor told me of her success in hiring a friend's teenage son to do the weekly grocery shopping which she felt burdened her day. The young man may not be eager to do the same chore in his own family, but when presented as "hire for pay," it represented spending money for him. A good idea and worth every cent for the freedom it gives her to balance the multifaceted role she is living.

Here is yet another thing she shared and one which you may wish to consider. She is a busy, full-time accountant. For the first few years, while her business was growing, she frequently attempted to pick up a few items from the neighborhood grocer on her way home from the office. Then, she timed herself and realized over two hours had been wasted in one week just standing in line. She was determined to find an efficient solution to grocery shopping. This is the system she developed and it can be tailored to suit many lifestyles.

> *Complete List:* A grocery list of items used regularly which show up on the list repeatedly. Note: A review of past buying habits will prove that most people buy the same items regularly and to prepare the list one time saves rewriting the same list over and over.

> *Half-List:* This list includes items picked up about every third day such as dairy and perishable salad ingredients, fruits of the season and special taste treats.

> *Party List:* This is a true motivator and will springboard a party into reality. The planning has been completed on paper. Taking a copy of the Party List, for instance, handing it to a friend who you'll be inviting to the party and who may have some spare moments to market when you do not, makes the selection of items from a check list a breeze.

The secret to this system working is the preplanning. It takes only a few minutes to xerox several copies of each grocery list. When you have several copies of the lists on hand you can delegate the chore to other family members or, like my neighbor, hire a responsible teenager to shop. Or an easy tradeoff can be arranged. For example, I know another woman who is a talented painter. She trades her delicate miniatures, a weekend hobby, to the friends who want them to give as gifts, and who, in turn, regularly shop for her. Develop a mutual system with another who has the time to shop and may even enjoy it. Picking up dual groceries is quite simple when the system has been established and a check list is followed. Of course, the opportunity of hiring someone relieves you of the task without incurring another obligation.

I can't think of a better way to use time you save than to throw a party. The inspiration of hosting a party is often suffocated because the planning and organization seem too demanding. The secret to entertaining easily is simple. Prepare for the party in advance of the date and continue to think about entertaining on a regular basis. Don't put off having friends in for a good time. To entertain freely and with minimum effort, it is essential to be prepared for instant parties. Dishes and coffee cups that stack easily for storage not far from reach allow you to use space to the maximum. In our home, the supplies are in the shelves under the stairs. The hall closet shelf holds the large punchbowl, many, many glasses and four dozen white cups which stack. These are excellent for hot soups served around the fireplace as a first course, for Tom and Jerry's, as well as the coffee and tea for which they were originally intended. Creative ideas stimulate interest and encourage new ways of entertaining. A traditional sit-down dinner is fine on occasion but less formal settings, potluck gatherings, picnics inside and out, barbecues when weather permits, inviting friends for brunch, or just dessert and coffee introduces an entirely different attitude about entertaining. Let go of habits that restrict you. We all enjoy exploring something new, and a hostess who is aware of this will have more fun than anyone at the party.

Once again, what does this have to do with *Getting Ready?* Everything. Changing the way you have been doing things is very difficult. It takes decision-making and determination to assure the success of a new lifestyle. Give it a try and you'll find the change will give you desire to reach out even further.

In Charlotte Towle's book, *Common Human Needs,* she speaks in rather complex terms about the results of this experience. "There is evidence in human behavior that, in contrast to the tendency toward resistance to change and regression to the past, there is also a strong and inevitable impulse toward progression. There is movement into new experience, giving of self to creative activity, giving of energy to work that serves a purpose beyond the objective of mere survival, giving of self in relationships that contribute to and gratify others as well as serve the purpose of self-gratification."

The feeling derived from sharing with others, inviting friends into your home, and experiencing the rapport and satisfaction of good hospitality, food and conversation is happiness.

Simplifying the ways in which you deal with food, supplies and storage will allow you the freedom to enjoy friends at leisure. Introducing this plan of action while you are still home much of the time will give you the practice to make the routine a habit. Later, when you are working away from home, the whole process of entertaining will have been placed in the correct perspective and will continue to be a very pleasant part of your life.

It is important to continue to work through the other rooms of your home, touching upon other areas that can be simplified and, as a result, offer more satisfaction. Look around your home and especially consider the things you have purchased or were purchased for you as the result of clever marketing. How many were based upon actual need? Each of the things brought into your home must have a place. A new appliance, large or small, demands a share of the territory. How often is it used? In your kitchen, does the array of miracle machines that promised to save time and provide freedom from cutting, chopping, blending, squeezing, and brewing really get used? How many of these implements are in need of repair but have stayed on, occupying prime space in your kitchen and continuing to mock and frustrate you?

Solution: Pick up that small 3-S notebook that you are carrying to record observations on how you really listen, what you hear, and who you meet . . . and make yourself a note to meet a repairman. Toss, recycle or sell the items that you agree must go.

Garage sales take effort but the cash is a nice reward for the work. It will be more fun if you join forces with others and divide the responsibilities for advertising, setup, selling, and cleaning up. A one-day sale can net proceeds you would not believe from items you are not using. But beware, the space you clear will become open territory and, like a magnet, will attract other possessions. Think of the many things you bring into the home almost daily. Consider the few times you removed any of them. Recycling cannot be an occasional practice; it has to be continual if you want order and open space.

You can quickly control a cluttered appearance in any particular place. In the family den, for example, by using a variety of containers—baskets, chests, hampers, and so on—to hold the pieces and parts of hobbies, sewing, projects, and anything that is *on hold.*

Are you a seamstress who has fallen victim to the paper bag syndrome? An article appeared in our morning San Francisco *Chronicle* with the headline, Why Working Women Find Time For Sewing. The report, by Jennifer Seder, explained a comment made by Susan Pletsch, who gives sewing seminars. Called the paper bag syndrome, it goes like this: You buy a pattern and some fabric, and you cut out the fabric and pin the pieces together. Then you take a break and fold up all the pieces and put them back in the bag, where they stay forever. Ms. Pletsch offers this worthwhile advice. "I tell my students always to sew together the major seams before taking that first break, and that way the whole thing is just too big to shove back in the bag."

For anyone who sews, a new trend is becoming apparent. Women are sewing today because they want the professional fit they can't seem to find otherwise. Robert Brown, advertising and sales promotion director of Simplicity, the nation's largest pattern company, says his firm's recent consumer survey shows more women would take up sewing if there were more convenient ways of learning the craft. To that end, Simplicity is sponsoring a pilot sewing class conducted after hours at a New York bank, and Brown says there is already a waiting list of two hundred people. The time and frustration spent searching through the excessive amounts of merchandise in every store just might be reduced considerably by considering the alternatives.

Investing the time to develop the skill necessary to produce a professional, well-fitting garment at half the price of its ready-to-wear counterpart could benefit you in another way. Dr. Roderic Gorney, a professor of psychiatry at UCLA, says sewing is good for our psyches. He goes on to state, "In prehistoric times, man used his hands to do everything. Now, most people work with their heads and are intimidated just to sew a hem. If we all did something with our hands just once, maybe we'd be better-balanced human beings." Give this some thought. Although my mother was an expert seamstress, I was never enthusiastic to learn. However, I plan to learn since I find my priorities are continually changing as I move through the various stages of life.

Just reading Dr. Gorney's statement that it's good for our psyches stimulated me to make a note in my 3-S notebook to check out available tailoring classes. The next step will be to carve out the time on a regular basis to take lessons, do the homework, and put the skill through the necessary steps.

We enjoy that which we do well, right? To start anything that you do not fully intend to follow through will fragment you with another "paper bag" project *on hold.* In order to simplify your life, continue to ask yourself *how?* How will doing this simplify my life? For me, in the case of sewing, the answer is to eliminate the distaste I have for searching and shopping and finding little that pleases me. I return from such an experience with negative feelings about poor quality and workmanship in readymade clothing. By reversing this and taking personal responsibility for resolving the problem, I shall be doing a great deal for my psyche, and for my budget.

Turning half-steps into profit will be covered more thoroughly in a later chapter; however, there is a great potential source of income for women who develop sewing and design skills in teaching others who are eager to learn the craft. For those of you reading this who are already accomplished seamstresses and enjoy the activity, start turning this talent into top dollar. Personal consultations, group classes, lecturing, and even writing are potential goals for you. Some of the first steps necessary to launch such ambitious plans are clearly outlined in the next chapters.

Assignments

1. Establish a Think Center for convenience and efficiency in managing the home. Handling so many responsibilities well requires executive organization and a desk is essential.

2. Supply the Think Center with all items necessary.

3. Practice using the A.F.T. (Action, File or Toss) system.

4. Create fat files versus skinny files for a workable file system.

5. Consider a clock radio if you do not have one at this time.

6. Purchase a timer to start the coffee brewing early.

7. Strategically post the grocery list and encourage all family members to contribute to it.

8. Replace old shopping habits with new and more productive ones.

9. Consider alternatives for dining and for entertaining.

10. Relieve the boredom of routine and strive for the joy of change.

11. List items needing repair in your 3-S book and plan a time when you will have everything repaired, replaced or recycled.

12. If you suffer from the paper bag syndrome of sewing, or of any project started and not completed, decide on a course of action. Fragmentation is a serious problem and compulsion to close is an important time management principle which should be closely observed.

Motivation Made Easy

The last chapter may have left you exhausted or refreshed, depending on how much of the assignment you decided to do and how the results affected you. The focus of *Getting Ready* is to help prepare the way for change. One is unable to bring about change if daily habits dominate each day. The best of intentions will never benefit you unless you actually change your routine. Making changes is not easy. Ninety percent of our behavior is based on conditioning and controlled by habit and that is difficult to alter. It takes real dedication to make positive changes in your life. The fact that you have read this far indicates that you possess self-discipline, a positive attitude, and the desire to do something terrific with your life.

Earlier I introduced the subject of positive thinking and how surrounding yourself with inspirational messages will influence your feelings of self-worth. Read a daily inspirational essay and practice the art of seeing life in the glow of sunshine. Through this you will be able to dismiss the gloom that too many are preaching.

Read again the suggestions for your personal growth and give an award to yourself for every goal achieved.

The decision to make changes or to complete desired goals is not easy when the days never seem to have enough hours in which to take care of life's basic needs. There is another category of priorities, and they are the important things you must not lose sight of. While life marches steadily forward day by day, it is imperative to keep future goals simmering on the back burner. But what is it that hinders us from picking up on the important things and taking the time to accomplish them? Wouldn't you agree it may be lack of motivation?

I heard a definition of character the other day that seems appropriate here: "Character is the ability to carry through an idea, long after the mood is gone." Strength of character is necessary to stir yourself and generate motivation to complete a project, to carry out a plan, and to realize goals.

For example, have you promised yourself you will go jogging early each morning and then find you search for an excuse to put off doing it another day? The extra sleep seems to win out. Perhaps an appointment to jog at a certain hour with a buddy, neighbor or family member will establish the right atmosphere to give you the necessary push. The key to carrying good intentions through to reality is to make them attainable. Choose only realistic goals. If you feel some doubt about your willingness to spend the morning hour jogging, look to an evening hour instead, or settle for another type of exercise. Do not weigh yourself down with a guilt trip! Do not put any task in front of you which is distasteful. Consider your own personal internal rhythm and work you goals into it. Not everyone is a day person and you may find your enthusiasm and energy is at its peak at night.

To help motivate you toward the important things you want to do, here is an ideal tool to help you to stay on the track—the color-coded index card file system. It serves as a quiet, persistent, and clever motivator.

Supplies you will need: Unlined index cards measuring 3″×5″. These cards are sold in stationery and office supply stores. Pick up a packet in each color—yellow, orange, blue, green and pink. Also, buy six medium-sized notebook rings and a paper punch.

Take three cards from each pack for a total of fifteen cards. Punch a single hole in the upper lefthand corner of each and place them on a notebook ring.

Flip the cards to the three yellow ones. These are Sunshine and Cheer Cards. Think of what awards you would like to give yourself: a special treat, a small luxury, a special pleasure. Anytime you think of an award you would like, turn to the yellow cards and write it down. Keep the ideas coming to motivate yourself for special awards.

Now turn to the three orange cards. They represent the first week of the month. List the special things you would like to accomplish the forthcoming week. This should not include the routine tasks that you must do such as errands, appointments, or grocery shopping. List the things you think about doing one day when you have enough time. For example: Have you been thinking about the artwork you did in college and how you would like to get back into the mood of drawing? And what is the reason you don't? Just can't seem to find the time?

First you need to create an atmosphere that will stimulate your desire to pick up your sketchbook. Create a special place for your art supplies. Arrange an attractive and comfortable sun-drenched corner of a room and stock it with your charcoal pencils, drawing paper, easel, and all the necessary equipment to support your creative urge. It is imperative to prepare for the moment you want to draw or paint without having to stop and start. Then you will be drawn into the mood.

The orange cards act as the voice that says, "O.K., buy the supplies this week." List everything you will need, including baskets and pretty holders to store the supplies for easy access. Add visual beauty by controlling the clutter of items by placing them in a variety of unorthodox containers. Clear mason jars make an attractive holder for brushes. A unit with a series of dowels can be constructed to hold large sheets of art paper which will utilize space and look attractive as well. Some hotels and libraries have similar units to hold newspapers.

Proper lighting is frequently overlooked in project areas. Your efforts are handicapped without the best and most appropriate type of light. On an orange card make a note to buy a draftsman's lamp that screws onto the table or bookshelf. You will be able to direct the light exactly where you want it. Ideal light for daytime will be in the sunny corner I mentioned earlier, but the sun doesn't always shine or you may not have a window spot available. It is important to do whatever is necessary to pursue your interests as a part of your everyday life.

In a later chapter we will see how half-steps have helped a number of women develop profitable careers, and you will see the importance of creating an appropriate setting. My suggestion of art was only an example. Come up with a single project or interest of your own. But only one. Do not overextend yourself by listing more than one project. Remember to note on one of the orange cards the supplies you will need to get started and be sure to pick up the items before the end of the week.

The blue cards represent the second week of the month. On the top blue card write in a realistic date as the deadline for getting your equipment set up and the corner you have selected ready for you to work. The same process can be carried out if you decide to take up sewing, sculpture, photography, writing or studying for any pursuit. One project is listed and the orange cards cover the first week's assignment. The blue cards then set the deadline you have given yourself to complete the next portion of the plan. The progress you would like to see yourself make by the end of the third week should be outlined on the three green cards.

Now that you are moving forward and feel the motivation to continue, recharge your energies by reaching for a yellow card. Listed on the card are some treats you would like to give yourself. Think of all you have done these past weeks. Surely you deserve an award!

A woman who attended one of my seminars covered her yellow card with "tourist suggestions." She would imagine herself a tourist and select something to see in the city, a special restaurant, a new art gallery, or a special show, and spend the hours enjoying the treat from the perspective of an out-of-towner. Her ultimate award was checking into a hotel and treating herself to the luxury of room service, breakfast in bed, and a full day to relax. The woman happened to be a single parent and needed a complete change of pace. She would arrange well in advance for her children's care, and check into a hotel within a few miles of her home. She feels the experience helped her through some very difficult times. Distance need not be equated with pleasure. Consider the very area where you live and look at it with the fresh awareness of a tourist. This may be an idea you will want to include on your yellow card. The list is limitless; just keep being good to yourself because it is reflected to all of those around you.

Let me pause here for a moment and ask if the personal improvement program included goals you are hoping to reach. Remember in the chapter on personal growth we spoke briefly about physical appearance? These color-coded cards can work as a noncritical friend to help remind you, for example, of the daily exercise program you promised yourself you would start. Still only promises? Still too busy each day? Jot "exercises" on a green card. The enthusiasm that you are now feeling after a couple of weeks involved in an exciting project will spill over to wanting to increase an overall program of progress. Unless the physical self is in good tune, the energy level will be low. Carrying excess weight demands more work of your heart and other organs and is a health concern to many. The guilt complex you may suffer because of excess weight can be overcome once you have achieved the self-discipline to eat half as much and exercise regularly. Support is perhaps your best ally in this effort. Join with others in a group or class, avail yourself of the excellent programs on television every morning, and work out with the experts. They look as they do because they block a definite time for exercise and do it daily. Also, they must perform on the shows because they are under contract to do so, and nothing really makes one do a job like a contract. Whichever way you choose, the results will give you pleasure. Make a notation on the green card now.

For the last week of the month, I want to make a suggestion for the pink cards. This comes also from a number of women who totally agree about the importance of a skill they feel is priceless. That is, *learning to type well.*

The ability to type has moved me along toward my long-range goals. I would never have realized this if I did not type. For just a moment I will share my experience with you. One of my best remembered toys was a play typewriter that had a miniature standard keyboard and really worked. I was ten years old, the occasion was Christmas, and I thought it was the greatest gift anyone could receive. The one-room rural school I attended did not offer a typing course. But I was fortunate because Miss Husmann, the schoolteacher, lived with our family and many long hours were available after school when I benefited from her personal tutoring. Encouraged by her typing skill, I soon mastered the small keyboard. Typing represented a sense of order and clarity for me.

When I think about that experience I believe it is why I chose business as my college major and continued to take a series of courses in support of business skills. I occasionally used the typewriter during my travel career; however, the unique opportunity to serve as National Secretary of the former stewardess alumnae group required real typing skills. I qualified and was elected to the National Kiwi Board. Later, promotion to National President required continual communication with hundreds of women who had previously flown for American Airlines. Typed letters communicate easily and alleviate the frustration of attempting to decipher handwriting. Without a doubt, it would have been impossible for me to have authored books or founded my time management consulting business if I had not been able to type. Currently, I personally correspond with many of my instructors, students, readers, and clients. I can chat with them daily by postcard and my typing skill keeps those cards moving along quickly. This personal testimony to the advantages of typing is to encourage you to put three small words on your pink card: "Learn to type" or "Improve my typing."

Start with a ten-minute typing exercise as a daily

routine. Within six months you will be proud of your typing skill. There are excellent books which provide all you need to develop this priceless skill. If you have doubt about just how important it really is, please ask any successful friend who types well how it has helped her. This is a direct quote from a woman who is the secretary to a Circuit Judge in Illinois. Barbara said, "If I had to list one single skill that I feel is my most important asset, I would say it is typing. Some women would disagree; however, I feel it has definitely led me toward other opportunities."

There is a myth that one should not type because it may trap you in a dead-end job. Tell me this, who is ever to know you type if you don't put it on your resume or tell them you can? If you prefer, keep it your secret, but don't deny yourself the control reflected by the professional appearance a neatly typed letter gives to the reader. It commands attention and instant respect. After verbal communication, a follow-up letter, typed on handsome stationery, will open a door that just might have remained closed if anything less was received. I can't make you want to change a belief you have held for a long time, but I do encourage you to consider the unlimited benefits it can provide. An added bonus will be the example set for your children. A typewriter in the home will inspire children to type their assignments, essays, and term papers. A typed paper is often graded higher and it will definitely give a sense of neatness to their work. The example I have set for our three children has resulted in each of them using the typewriter regularly. Today, our daughter in college is grateful to have typing skills to help her keep up with the enormous demands of education. Our son, a high school senior, is able to turn out twice the amount of work. The thoughts are transmitted onto the typed page automatically. That isn't as easy when attempting to hand write every word. It is obvious I could go on and on about the benefits of this simple skill. It is only because I want you to experience the clarity it can give to your daily routine. Put those three words on your pink card and spend ten minutes practicing each day until you master the skill of typing.

Here is an extra bonus for the last week of the month. Think about other ways you might simplify your life. Consider giving up the morning newspaper habit. Do you spend from ten minutes to a half-hour poring over the paper? How about a half-hour run or brisk walk instead, and then listening to the news on the radio or television while you continue your morning routine? We are caught up in the morning newspaper habit because it has been around longer. The news reports on radio and television are constantly updated, so let the experts bring the news to you and you can spend the time to better advantage.

We operate from a strong base of doing things out of habit. This conditioning makes it very difficult to change from the old ways to something new. It is certain to be awkward. Even after one or two days of change we very often slip back to old habits before the week goes by. A new habit must be repeated at least twenty-one times before you have a chance of adopting it as part of your lifestyle. So why not set the goal for a full twenty-one days? Whatever you would like to change can be helped along with the simple system of using your color-coded cards on a notebook ring. It is a very basic system that is void of anything complex, confusing or costly. What do you have to lose? Or, more important, what do you have to gain? Think of the advantages in avoiding procrastination, doing away with the "if" and the "maybe." Just take hold of those reins and say out loud, "Why not?"

This motivational tool will help you focus on the important things in your life. Each day winds down to become another memory, and too often there are many things one just doesn't get done. Life is precious and too brief to be caught in the web of such frustration. When you begin using this system regularly you will build a healthy pattern of completing the things you have been putting off. The cards will give you the direction and discipline necessary to say a courteous "no" to many requests which are not your own first priorities.

Take the time to be good to yourself by increasing the number of award ideas on your yellow cards. Reach for the sunshine anytime you are feeling down or need a spark to keep going. A proper balance in one's life demands play as well as work. Schedule only as many things each day as you can comfortably complete, and stop attempting to do everything for everyone.

The cards are you friend and will help you find the smile in every day.

Assignment

1. Purchase five packets of color-coded index cards: yellow, orange, blue, green and pink, six notebook rings, and a paper hole punch.

2. Assemble the cards into groups of three of each color with the notebook ring.

3. Fill the yellow cards with Sunshine (award time) suggestions.

4. Follow the examples of how each color card is used through the month. Be realistic in putting down only those things you can complete. Keep the projects, ideas, and goals moving along every week.

5. Write in pencil, so necessary changes can be made easily and there is not a crossed out project to make you feel guilty for not going through with it. Be free to change and accept it readily because, remember, it does indeed take courage to change.

Half-Steps

Half-steps are a disciplined use of time each day to concentrate on a desired goal. Women are caught in a seemingly innocent trap when their day is fragmented. Starting with one thing and being drawn into another, and still another, simply results in not getting back to complete the first thing you started. When the entire day moves along like this and nothing is completed, the feeling of inadequacy and the frustration you suffer is stressful. Fragmentation is an insidious condition. The symptoms are often hidden and the prognosis uncertain. The problem grows out of proportion, restlessness develops, and a woman begins to question where she is going and who she is.

The half-step program I introduced in my time management book offered many suggestions for starting work on an interest or hobby in the home. For convenience, I used the alphabet as a sequential guide and to stimulate the imagination toward other possible interests that could be developed.

Art, Antiques and Alterations were the first few starting with A. By exploring the various opportunities under each category, we find there are many alternatives for everyone. This exercise of thinking about many options you might want to consider is a definite first step toward *Getting Ready*. The half-step program will help you to do that while protecting your own private time and personal moments. The woman who has chosen to stay at home must often defend her right to privacy. If this is your way of life at the moment, consider developing a professional half-step program in your home. By working regularly on this apprenticeship you will prepare yourself for the time you may choose, or possibly need, to enter into full-time gainful employment. Plans made now will assure your doing that on your own terms.

The focus of *Getting Ready* is toward taking slow but steady steps each day in order to have personal and professional insurance for the future. We cannot foresee what next month, or even next week, may bring in our lives. To continue in the same naive pattern simply isn't good business. Alert and intelligent women today are aware of how quickly their lives can change. The courage to take stpes to be prepared for change reflects maturity. In today's world one must take responsibility for one's life and make the best use of time. Understanding the importance and logical sequence of these exercises will provide the enthusiasm and excitement to motivate you to get ready for the career you want.

Earlier chapters explained the importance of preparing the mind for change, creating a distinct awareness and sensitivity for those people you meet, and starting the habit of keeping a 3-S notebook to build contacts for a later time. You were encouraged to clear some space to allow yourself the freedom to house new projects and, possibly, the introduction of this half-step program. Using the color-coded index card system is a motivational tool to help structure the time to develop your talents and interests. This pacing of each day will prepare you for the time you may wish to pursue a career that will use your own special aptitudes in the best possible way.

Two problems seem to hang heavy for the person working at home—clear direction and lack of time. This chapter is devoted to sharing some successful experiences of others. Perhaps they will give you some ideas which will propel you into new pursuits or provide the stimulus to get you actively making plans for the future.

Susan, the young mother of two preschoolers, was expecting her third child when she came to attend one of my workshops on time management. She had serious doubts that anyone could find time for her to spend in any way other than with babies, diapers, and formulas. However, she was willing to give full attention to the workshop and her attitude was one of readiness to change.

I stressed to the group the importance of keeping a small, simple, spiral notebook, and explained that eighty-five percent of the jobs in this country are filled through personal contacts. All the classified ads, employment agencies, and professional search firms account for only fifteen percent of job placement. If contacts are that important, it seems picking up a new contact should be a daily goal. The assignment was to buy a 3-S notebook and practice the concentrated listening exercise with three people each day. They were to enter the names and thoughts about them for possible future reference.

The following week, Susan returned to the group with

great enthusiasm and a notebook containing far more names than had been suggested. She explained it was her new awareness that opened her to so many more conversations with people in the neighborhood, at the corner grocery, the cleaners, and even people she met at the park. The class worked together through the guidelines for handling housework and preparing their personal system for controlling time spent on necessary duties in the home. Many were eager to know more about the half-step program they had read about at the end of the text. In this particular case, Susan again became the star pupil at the next class session. I suggested thinking about the half-step plan for the coming week and perhaps making a decision about something they would like to develop into a paying business. Susan, our young mother of soon to be three, reached back to her advanced skill in calligraphy and realized she had potential clients listed in her 3-S notebook. Taking a chapter from my time management book, she had the professional letterhead, envelopes, postcards and business cards printed for herself. In beautiful script they stated:

Susan Higgins
Calligraphy specialist

It took only three days to get her cards printed, and the day she picked them up she took a handful and visited ten of the people listed in her little contact book. Six of them gave her orders almost immediately, one for invitations to an open house, a special thank you letter, and for a single poem. Others placed orders for Christmas instead of buying commercial cards. Susan's creative mind gave each of them ideas for how they would benefit by using a personal message done in calligraphy. They recognized the individual touch this would give to anything they wanted printed and, with a conservative price list to start, the customers were eager to buy. Susan shared every step of her marketing plan with the group and by the next class session three more women had followed the identical program and developed their own unique skills, had stationery printed, and sold the product to contacts listed in their 3-S notebooks.

This may sound too simple. Perhaps it was only a coincidence that a single idea should have triggered a chain reaction; however, the elements necessary for a business were all available: clients, product, professional appearance, creative marketing plan, and the fire of ambition that was within each woman. They believed they could—and they did.

Sara was eager for a part-time job that would fill the void after the last of her seven children left for school. She had been so busy for years caring for them that the routine of always being busy was part of her personality. Searching for something she really enjoyed doing, Sara singled out the joy of cooking as her target. The first assignment she gave herself was to draw up a list of all the gourmet cookware shops in her area. It is important to determine on a map the area in which you want to concentrate, within the proximity of your home, to assure you do not spend wasted hours commuting. For many, excellent opportunities are within minutes of home, as in Sara's case.

While visiting the third shop on her list she shared with the owner some of her background experience. In less than ten minutes the owner asked Sara to come in for a couple of hours two mornings a week and show other women the techniques she had developed over the years for preparing meals for her family of seven. The interest grew and soon Sara was working four mornings a week. She loves to share her knowledge and enjoys the support she receives from the audience. Because the presentation took such a brief time, it was ideal for the part-time work she wanted.

When I last spoke with Sara she was considering

opening a gourmet shop of her own one day. It may be a long time down the road; however, the experience has served as a business course for her and provided her with confidence and practical on-the-job training. Never would she have considered something so awesome if it had not been introduced in manageable segments. Sara had thought of herself as a woman who possessed few skills of value in the job market. Suddenly, she realized her life experience was valuable and every skill she used as wife, mother, and homemaker could be applied to organizing, communicating, selling, and planning that she was doing on the job. Many women find this to be the case. Many times they are unaware until someone comes along and says, "Hey, you have a great deal to offer. Have you ever thought about . . .?" Whatever is mentioned just might become a special opportunity. Open your eyes to the possible half-steps you may want to pursue.

This is another true story including a long-range plan for the woman and how she realized a profitable career that she could balance with home, family, and husband. Kathleen was one of my early students and it was many years ago when she asked me over to her home for a cup of coffee and personal counseling. As we sat in her attractive living room, her two active preschoolers were demanding her attention and causing her to feel awkward about all the interruptions. Assuring her that I had three children, I explained how a fresh attitude toward one's life and blessings can happen when a personal interest helps to balance the day. Growing in a personal and professional manner adds new dimensions to days that are crowded with young children and little adult communication. Sometimes it takes another's objective comment to stir the obvious emotions about those closest to us.

Kathy had tears in her eyes when she looked up and

confessed she felt guilty for wanting time for herself away from the children so she could continue her study of art. The dream she held in secret was to have her very own graphic design studio. Some days she was sure it was only a dream and would never become a reality. I helped Kathleen try out a plan.

Ten minutes every day would be focused on building contacts. A walk with the children would include meeting people. Each day she would listen carefully and note the conversations in the 3-S notebook, including names and phone numbers for later reference. Her new manner of listening and really hearing people would provide many future contacts. Many would become her clients. People notice those who listen and care about them.

Kathleen had a special skill and was not aware of it at the time. Her artistic ability was reflected throughout her home. I remember saying to her, "Kathy, you are blessed with these two beautiful children, a husband who adores you, and a great talent. Look at how you have turned this house into a lovely home. Every home on this block looks quite alike on the outside, but it is what you have achieved with a few yards of fabric, some wallpaper and touches of art that have made the difference." For example, she had covered a small end table next to the sofa and used the same fabric to create a three-panel screen. The cost of the material was modest but her creative talent resulted in monetary savings and had given her a feeling of personal pride. "How many women," I asked, "could benefit by hearing you share this information and showing them how to do something similar?"

Kathleen quickly agreed she knew at least a dozen who had asked how she did a number of things in her home. Her modesty had kept her answers brief and she had not considered the marketing potential.

I explained the purpose of the half-step program and

suggested she pace herself slowly, especially during the time her young children were at home. In a surge of enthusiasm Kathy was asking me how and where and did I really believe she could do it and still care for her family.

I assured her that balance could be achieved and both she and her family could benefit. There is an increased awareness of personal identity when a mother is also improving her skills each day. The family starts to take on individual responsibility which is essential for their own growth and development. A fresh respect for one another is an added bonus.

Today, Kathleen spends hours in her graphics studio and calls on clients while her youngsters are in school. She manages to be home well ahead of them and her number one priority is still, and she believes will always be, her husband, family, and home. But it was the early half-step program of teaching interested women a simplified course in decorating on a shoestring that allowed Kathleen to build the cash reserve she needed to open her graphics studio.

Any woman at home raising a family is given a daily opportunity to explore creative activities. Consciously setting aside a space in every day allows her the chance to explore many artistic activities. Society has labeled an activity one enjoys as leisure, a hobby. The good news about the word "hobby" is that the moment you change the title to "profession" you activate cash flow. Your hobby starts to generate dollars and you are busy having a great deal of "fun" while making "funds."

Countless thousands of women are talented in the skill of arts and crafts items. Their apprenticeship is served over many years of church and school fund raising bazaars. Potential personal profits are never realized because of the initial fear of risk-taking and summoning the courage to show the work to retail stores.

For any of you reading this and knowing you have talent, and samples of your work, I encourage you to follow the example of Jennifer. I met Jennifer following a sorority tea. She came up to me after my presentation and explained she felt like an exact copy of the young mother I had described in my program. When I mentioned the name of the person, Jennifer squealed with delight. It was a sorority sister she had known while in college and majoring in chemistry. The ironic thing about this coincidence was that both women had been trained in the sciences and had never thought of themselves as having artistic aptitudes. When they individually followed their own drummer, husband and family priorities had put their aspirations of being another Madame Curie to rest. Their individual pursuits had shown a marked similarity during the years they had not been in contact. Activity in church and school projects gave them the opportunity to develop creative capabilities that had been dormant too long. Both women found doing things at home on their own time schedule exhilarating following the years of restrictive hours and study. A taste of pottery making for one and jewelry design for the other resulted in their pursuing additional classes and soon they were marketing their products. Jennifer couldn't wait to compare notes with her friend. The last time I spoke with her, the two of them were planning to open a jewelry and gallery boutique.

Too often we read about the success of another and rationalize that we don't have a sorority sister to meet after years of silence and, consequently, the goal of opening any business seems a distant dream. The unknown may be coupled with fear and caution, but don't allow them to control your life and rob you of the excitement you'll experience with a self-fulfilling career. If you possess the ability to create marketable arts and crafts, plan to call for interviews to show your work. What is the worst thing that can happen if you show what you can do to the buyer of specialty items in a large department store? Your request that they take some of the work on consignment is an offer you should make with great pride. Your attitude and assertiveness will create the positive climate necessary to assure a positive answer to your suggestion. Prepare your questions in advance and attempt to phrase them so the buyer will verbally answer "yes" to the questions you ask. For example: "Are your customers eager to buy original pieces of art?" The "yes" answer to this direct question is an ideal opening for you to show the line of quality art objects you have brought to display. Allow him or her to describe the types of customers and concentrate carefully during the explanation. Develop a comment about your type of art that distinctly relates the customer described to the kind of art you produce. Become sensitive to the market and target your merchandise to the select area you believe is your best customer.

If space and time allowed, I would like to list countless success stories. In conclusion, I will tell you about a personal friend of many years who is the founder and president of a thriving firm she has called House of Color. Karen had been a kindergarten teacher for years before her first child came along. She retired from teaching and developed her interest in drawing and painting during the hours her little one napped. She first started with dime store water colors and worked her way to acrylics and oils. As her daughter grew, Karen's teaching instinct surfaced and soon she was showing six of her daughter's friends the fun that painting and drawing could be for them. The structure of a nursery school situation with pure emphasis on the arts was the next step, and as the years flew by Karen started teaching other mothers the skills she had learned, and which she continued to improve through a series of art classes at the museum. The last time I spoke with Karen she was training an associate to open a second House of Color in a neighboring town. The future looks very promising and Karen continues the smooth rhythm in her life by doing a little each day toward her goals, being careful at all times to not become too busy or fragmented. Karen is acutely aware of how easily an activity can take control of one's life. She has witnessed too many superwomen, and her emphasis is on moderation of activity so that it serves her, rather than allowing herself to become subservient to it.

These experiences of others relate only a few testimonies of those who have found half-steps work. Every day that slips by is another twenty-four hours of lost opportunity, and none of us can afford to let those days slip by and be lost forever.

Visual - Verbal
(Keys to Careers)

We have many things to accomplish together and by doing a small amount each day we will make steady progress. Don't be discouraged if you seem to be slipping backward some days. Life often appears so complicated that it is difficult to know where to start any change in what could or should be done. When you feel like that, try my personal plan for a good starting place. The trick is to not to attack a huge project but to break it apart into smaller, more meaningful pieces. Here is an illustration that I use for clients who are frustrated by their own procrastination and have decided to make some changes in order to focus on goals they want to achieve.

Imagine yourself entertaining a group of neighborhood women who have dropped by your home in the late afternoon for a committee meeting to plan a weekend block party. After an hour of concentrated discussion and suggestions, you offer each a glass of wine. Thinking about an appetizer you might serve, you excuse yourself, go into the kitchen and take a salami from the sideboard. Now, what do you do? You could take it to the living room and place it on the glass coffee table in front of your guests. However, I suspect that when you sat down once more to continue the conversation you might sense the women looking at the coffee table, glancing at you, and then back to the food, totally intimidated by it. And rightly so. Obviously, nothing will be done about a large piece of meat encased in heavy plastic and resting on a glass coffee table.

Instead, while in the kitchen, you take a really sharp knife and carefully slice the salami into paper thin slices. You then wrap each slice around a sliver of gherkin pickle, quickly arrange the appetizers on a lovely china plate, and return to serve your guests an easily handled tidbit. The point of this story is that we must take care to pace our day to include only a reasonable amount of responsibility in order that it can be handled in a way that is not awkward. The huge salami was intimidating by its very size and packaging. Taking control simply involved removing the outer casing, slicing pieces which could be easily digested, and enjoying the end result.

Consider this a visual lesson in structuring a portion of each day toward growth that is vital to your control and confidence. Every day provides an opportunity for growth toward a future goal. I am thoroughly aware of the demands on your time, but it seems realistic to invest ten minutes each day.

That ten minutes of concentrated time should be used to prepare a plan of action for when you feel ready to step out into the career search arena. The exercises suggested earlier were planned chronologically to arrive now on the threshold of getting the job you want. Let's start with the tools you have been developing.

To improve the effectiveness of your 3-S notebook, you should start to plan the direction and purpose of the contacts you will pursue. They are going to support the new interest that you are just developing. Your fledgling interest may be the life career of the person you are meeting, and the conversation may offer you great insight and an invaluable learning experience. For example, you may be talking to one of the owners of a small advertising agency. During the conversation you learn about the origins of the company, their marketing efforts and plans for future growth. You listen with great interest while the person tells you the reason why he or she left a big agency, a giant in the industry, to join a smaller office. And how did you happen to be talking to someone in a small advertising agency? Possibly to obtain information about having business cards and stationery designed. Occasionally it helps to give coincidence a small push in the right direction. In any event, a few statements made by someone in the business may provide the base from which you can gather additional material. For what reason? Because jobs in the media involve contact with people and you may really like working with people. That just happens to be the oft quoted response to the question, "What do you like to do?" The answer continues to be, "work with people." In order to best utilize your personal skills, control commute time, and just about write your ideal job description, it is essential to utilize all the inside tracks and research every avenue available to you. In the next chapter we will talk about compiling a personal resume, the A.B.E chart, which I have developed and tailored to showcase your special skills. It reflects the Ability, Background and the Experience you possess. You may not realize all of the skills you have—right now. Preparing your very own A.B.E. chart may uncover some surprises for you. For example, perhaps you have been a "people person" from the time you started working on the church newspaper and convincing merchants to buy ads. Gathering community support through contributions to the annual Project Fair sponsored by a local youth group each year further polished your approach. The years spent talking with people and getting results is experience that can now be transferred to the marketplace. Why not sell the services of a small ad agency to the many potential clients just waiting to hear about the firm?

Now I can almost hear you say, "Oh, I could never do that. Ad agencies require a college degree for such a position and I haven't been in school for twenty years." True, but everyone is not just out of school, and not everyone is going to have an M.B.A., extensive marketing background, or be a whiz in economics or math. Stop thinking of the things you may not have—think about the strength you *do* possess. The progression of this plan is toward getting ready for the day when you will feel prepared, and your A.B.E. chart will help provide the confidence and poise to show others that you have a great deal to offer. Cavett Robert is a marvelous man who continues to share words of wisdom with those who listen to his speeches, cassettes, and seminars. He often says, "*It takes contacts to make contracts.*"

I am convinced that those people who wish for ideal jobs and long for special careers are only as far away from their goal as they are willing to practice the two vital V's that make the difference.

Being *visual* and *verbal* will make the difference. How many times have you seen a friend, co-worker, relative, and perhaps even yourself, hide behind written correspondence or the telephone hoping that doors would open to a career? Mailing resumes is a game that frequently brings disappointment and rarely success.

Richard Nelson Bolles, in his career manual, *What Color Is Your Parachute?*, refers to sending out large numbers of resumes as the "numbers game." He goes on to report that some companies receive as many as 25,000 resumes a year. Even smaller companies receive as many as ten to fifteen a week. By mailing a resume, you put yourself in a stack with all the other resume senders who are playing the numbers game. For a moment, visualize how you would feel if you were sitting at a desk stacked high with applications and each day's mail brought more. How would you go about sorting through them? The word "eliminate" is used frequently as the solution to reducing the stack to a more manageable level.

Do me a favor. Anytime you start to hesitate about seeing a person versus hiding behind the safety of a letter or a phone call, focus your imagination on the stacks of written applications, resumes, and introductory letters that are mailed by those playing the numbers game.

You may believe that those in the business of uncovering the ideal jobs know the system and can help you. For a fee, the search firms, private career counselors, and even employment agencies, will help you play the numbers game. They will mail hundreds of letters but the replies you get may simply be a request for more information, an explanation that they aren't hiring at this time, or an expression of their regret—and, they may keep you on file.

According to studies of people who have tried the numbers game, for eighty to ninety-five percent it simply doesn't work. What does it do? It lowers a person's confidence and expectations. At a time when support and encouragement are most needed, the numbers game can cause an applicant to think something must be wrong with her. *Not so:* The vicious circle has trapped the victim.

Solution: Become visual and verbal.

Becoming visual and verbal means people contact. Leave your shyness on the top shelf of your hall closet and walk out that front door. Practice becoming visual and verbal in front of as many potential employers as you have planned for the day's quota.

Consider these facts from a study conducted by the Department of Labor. Thousands of job holders were asked how they found employment and their answers are included here for you.

Private employment agencies	1%
Public employment agencies	3%
Help wanted ads	5%
School placement services	6%

Only 15% attributed their employment to the above systems. How did the others land their jobs? By being visual and verbal!

Direct contact with employers. Going to them and asking for a job. Ask yourself what is the worst that can happen if you do this, and what is worst if you do not?	24%
The largest number of job applicants found positions through personal leads and introductions. Friends, family, and other relatives proved helpful.	48%
The remaining group listed a combination of the above methods to find a job.	13%

A term one hears a great deal in searching for career change or job opportunities is the "hidden job market." Richard Nelson Bolles explains that most people believe the only jobs available are those vacated by someone else. This is a basic mistake.

I want to encourage you to reverse the procedure and,

first of all, select the organization, the company, the location, and the atmosphere you prefer. Do not try to force your skills to fit into just any type of vacancy. Seek the place you want to work first. The next step is to unearth the problems your target company may be having and think of ways you can help them solve those problems. The position you carve out for yourself is the one the company will suddenly decide they need you to fill. In summary, creation of new positions is the key to the professional job market. Author Bolles explains, "One third of today's jobs didn't exist ten years ago."

True, it will take some imagination to create the job you want. For example, consider the executive whose ad agency is ready and eager to expand but has not been able to attract new accounts. Then, one morning you walk into the office, indicate your interest and genuine concern, outline your plan, and offer your contacts and the skills you possess which are directly related toward attracting the types of accounts the employer has been seeking. The result will be an offer for you to fill the position. The homework you did and your awareness of the timing and techniques that would work pays off in a top award. The job you wanted is yours.

The hidden job market focuses on the corporate world. In contrast, take a moment to think of how you might use the same plan to uncover a part-time job within a few blocks of your home. A new catering service may have just opened and money is obviously being spent on ads in the local newspapers and for distribution of flyers in the neighborhood. However, as you keep watching, the business has not really taken off. The problem is the need for a person who is visual and verbal. Could you see yourself walking into the manager's office, explaining your idea to increase their business by catering to women's organizations and school groups? Perhaps you have the unique background of knowing dozens of women's organizations and of having served on a number of their boards. You recognize the business they could give a new caterer. The personal introduction is missing and you are offering to make this essential link. Salary may be a problem for a fledgling business with cash flow difficulties, so consider offering to work on a commission for the first few months and negotiate your salary at the end of that time.

Your offer will probably result in an enthusiastic manager willing to give it a try. The next move is back in your ballpark. This is when all procrastination stops and you start planning on the people you will contact. You assemble a calendar and, supplied with menus, brochures, price list and business cards, you start scheduling appointments. Try to pace yourself to complete four calls each day for the first week. At the end of a five-day work week you will have reached twenty potential clients. Your carefully targeted audience will probably result in selling to a third of them, and some promises from others. The enthusiasm you have for what you are doing and the excitement it generates in the new caterer will turn out to be mutually rewarding. You can readily see the fine future this arrangement holds. At the end of three months you will be in a strong position to ask for a comfortable salary and still plan your own hours and working conditions.

Sound to good to be true? Not at all . . . the secret is in being visual and verbal. Nothing will hold an individual back more than hiding behind something that prevents the opportunity to be *seen and to be heard.* The selling power of those two assets is greater than all the resumes, degrees, and references you could possibly produce. Because there will be times when it is important to leave a resume with someone to whom you have spoken, the next chapter will undertake how to highlight your strong Ability, Background and Experience skills and present them with the importance they deserve.

A.B.E.
(Your Resume)

You may feel there is no reason to prepare an A.B.E. chart at this time. However, the convenience of having this unique tool ready when a special opportunity occurs and you want it quickly is sufficient reason to work along with this exercise and *do it now.*

I have terrific news for you! If you have spent the past years performing hundreds of tasks and projects involved in raising children, caring for your home and husband, the executive ability you have developed, when properly applied, is very marketable.

The A on the A.B.E. chart stands for Ability and executive skills, all of which are exceedingly desirable.

Executive Ability To:	*Homemaker, Mother and Wife*
Handle people	Daily nurtures, supports, referees and encourages.

Executive Ability To:	*Homemaker, Mother and Wife*
Establish important priorities	Daily schedules are a must in managing a household effectively.
Delegate authority and responsibility	Delegation of tasks teaches responsibility to the young.
Make decisions	The homemaker makes constant decisions daily, many on short notice.
Budget	Daily purchases demand a close budget for home, food and clothing.
Project long range plans	Planning for vacation, investments, personal goals and later years.
Communicate effectively.	Ability to communicate is the secret to a happy home and the skill is practiced constantly by the wife, mother and homemaker

The B for Background will include some interesting memories and it is going to be fun to recall the best of your successes on paper. There is a distinct power in the feeling of accomplishment. The energy one uses to do something well can be generated over and over again to repeat the success. Self-confidence grows from the memory of successful accomplishments.

O.K., are you ready to put on paper some of your glorious moments of success? Do not be alarmed if the page is still blank after several minutes. There are possible reasons for drawing a blank. Basically, we don't give ourselves enough credit for the things we do well. Instead, our attention is directed toward the failures and mistakes that load us down with guilt and grief. This is obviously not true of everyone. However, if a blank paper is still staring up at you, take another five minutes to reach way back in your memory. Recall the lead you had in the school play and the thrill of success you felt when you heard the applause. Or the high school debate team that went to a state contest, and won! Remember the success you felt when the judges announced the winners and you walked up to receive the award. After marriage, you and your husband joined a small dramatics club and the thrill of applause still rings in your ears, even these many years later. Those memories would suggest you enjoy an audience. You probably will not find excitement behind a desk where there is little contact with the public. "Skills" is another term that describes the accomplishments in one's background. The skills you used to achieve success are the same ones you can utilize in future work that will be most satisfactory. It is important here to first identify the success memory and uncover those skills associated with it.

Although you should be aware of your skills, don't allow them to become the determining factor in what type of work you choose. It is possible to have been trained to be an educator and then to find the classroom a difficult place for you. The confinement of one room and the repetition of the same subject is not stimulating for many, even though they graduated as teachers. My initial plan to become a teacher took a reverse turn when I realized these very points. As a result, I searched until I found a career so enjoyable that I could scarcely believe a paycheck was included. When one can turn the pleasure of work into a paid career, the very best of all things happen.

I had known it would be important to stay in the field

of helping others and I was good at guiding, teaching and listening to everyone—friends, acquaintances and total strangers. The opportunity to travel and to help many people with a variety of needs and concerns was part of my airline stewardess career, and it fit my expectations beautifully. The excitement of receiving a telegram informing me of my employment with an overseas airline was a moment I reflect upon often—as I have today. The excitement of international travel was fantastic. Those years provided a strong foundation of experience and developed skills which I transferred easily into my marriage and the raising of our children. Each step along the way is a learning experience and it is my purpose in this book to recognize the value of those assets and how they may be applied to the current job market.

It may be awhile before you recognize the enormous resources you have stored in the past. However, when you are ready for the first interviews, the homework you have completed will prepare you to consider your choice of careers. Put away any fear you may feel. It will only serve to hold you back. Confidence and poise are your strong assets.

There is a purposeful absence here of charts, graphs, forms, and the references to other works which tell you about success. All you need to succeed is yourself, a professional looking resume as a record of what you have done, and the confidence to sell yourself to the person capable of making decisions. This is a very important point: The person responsible for making decisions is the individual you will want to concentrate on seeing. Energy and time is wasted in dealing with anyone other than that individual. Locate the right person and always go directly to them.

The E on the chart will list the Experience you have had in the area in which you are looking for work. Be sure to present every item on the chart in a positive manner and avoid listing any education you received more than ten years ago. Focus upon the life experiences instead. A professionally prepared A.B.E. chart will outline your assets to your best advantage. Never be intimidated by one of the archaic employment applications that seem to be everywhere. You can fill in the form they give you with the usual name, address, phone, and questions particular to the firm or company but take along your A.B.E. resume and attach it. The unique credentials produced by life experience qualify the applicant for great job and career changes that no one else perceives until they are shown the logic of translating the skills. The years of volunteer job experiences serve as apprenticeship training. You must translate your skills into the vocabulary that is understood and in demand by those in a position to hire qualified people.

Never use the words "just" or "only." You are not *only* a homemaker, you are not *only* a mother, wife, housekeeper, whatever title you select. Never even think of yourself in the category of "not having worked." A homemaker works longer hours and develops many skills which are exceedingly marketable. Think in terms of the work you have done and how much of it is identical to the type of work an employer must pay to have done. Review the first page of this chapter again and see how the professional responsibilities of an executive apply to you.

Crisis management is a daily experience in an active home with children, their friends, the neighbors' youngsters, and interruptions all day. Are you the one who is continually calming the waters? Of course you are, and you have been doing so for years. Translating the skills used in handling disputes, anger, misunderstanding, and temper is your objective. Putting on paper, in the vocabulary used in the business world, and selling the person who is interviewing you that your abilities, background, and experience serve to qualify you for the position you want—that is your goal. Think of the skill you developed over the years in planning schedules so everyone had free time to enjoy family trips together. That role can be translated into a counseling, planning, and scheduling role in public relations. Choose your goal and go after it because you have been practicing the skills necessary to succeed for a long while.

It will be up to you to show the prospective employer how this constant rehearsal has educated you in the art of organization and planning. If your A.B.E. chart reflects your qualifications and if you are visual and verbal in your presentation of the things you do well, how can you miss?

Think for a moment about your last chairmanship of a school fund raiser. You were in charge of public relations, media contact, copywriting, scheduling, marketing, selling, delegating, and, when it was over, the final written report for the next year's chairman to study and use as a guide. You had committees to help you; however, as chairman, the final responsibility was really yours. Right? Be sure to include all of this experience when you prepare your A.B.E. chart. Do not try to hurry through it because you will miss a wealth of important information if you do. Much of it is buried in your subconscious and it will take you a while to start thinking in a positive manner and recall all the good experience you have had. It is not easy to start outlining one's successes when little has been said about them by anyone else. Homemakers and volunteers do not tend to attract the strokes and standing ovations they so richly deserve. Consequently, putting together the information will take some effort in attaining the right perspective to your achievements. Give your main objective some thought now because before the chart is ready, one single sentence must be included to summarize what it is you want to do. Until that question is answered, the interview, the search, the final decision is difficult to make.

I recently worked with a client named Sandra and helped her prepare an A.B.E. chart. Sandra was searching for part-time work in which she could become involved and feel needed. Her youngest child had just left for college and the eldest was married and lived on the East Coast. Sandra explained that her husband was a physician and deeply involved in his practice and outside research projects. While raising her family, Sandra had contributed much of her time to involvement with schools and churches. She helped with many fund raising projects, prepared food, chaired committees, and held offices, all of which gave her a feeling of self-worth. While we talked, she spoke briefly about the work she had done on the church newspaper. I asked her to bring along some of the articles she had written. Her material was exceptional and I learned that the church newspaper had finally become solvent through Sandra's efforts to sell ads, prepare copy, write feature articles, interview, and negotiate with suppliers and printers for their lowest rates.

It was not apparent to Sandra that she possessed any marketable skills. In fact, her confidence was at an all-time low when she came to me because of the embarrassment she had incurred earlier in the week.

This is the story she told me: After great effort, she had pulled together her courage to call for interviews at two employment agencies. The insensitive personnel clerks had caused Sandra to feel helplessly lost in a maze of routine application forms and questions about her recent job experience. She told me how she stared at the large blank space that required her to list her education, starting with the most recent and working backward. Sandra, like so many other women of her generation, had married after a year and a half of college. She felt so inadequate that afternoon that she excused herself and fled from the office. In just a few brief hours this lovely, capable, sensitive, and intelligent woman felt defeated and ready to give up her goal of working part-time for a salary. As she explained to me, "I was only testing myself to see if just maybe some of the things I had been doing without pay for so long could be used in the marketplace."

The good news and happy conclusion to this incident is to report that Sandra prepared an excellent A.B.E. chart, located a firm she knew through a personal contact, and is now working as an editorial assistant. A promotion is due soon. Sandra is bursting with excitement and keeps repeating how great it is to be paid for her efforts. She is working less and enjoying it more. The fragmentation of mothering, managing a home, and juggling other responsibilities is now gone. Her energies are focused on her career when she is away from home. When at home, her full attention is given to her husband, her home and herself.

The years of service and of giving are the price paid by all of us who have done volunteer work. The important truth is that during the time one is doing the giving, it satisfies many areas of need. Obviously, the cause is an important one and the ability to help gives personal satisfaction. Additionally, when one has young children, social sharing and the sense of belonging become important to every mother. As the years pass, many causes lose intensity as they are turned over to others. This is the first indication that it's time to move along, widen your interests, and start the search for where you want to be in the coming years. To really recognize the importance of a planned program of personal and professional growth, it may be essential to complete the experiences I have just described. Many times we are unable to look further ahead than we can actually see. I urge you to think about what you may be doing in ten years. Imagine where each of your family members will be at that time. It is vitally important to consider what your image will be when others are not the center of your attention. For those of you without the responsibility of children, I urge you to avoid any further delay. If your 3-S notebook is working for you, if the color-coded index cards have been incorporated to simplify your daily routine, much progress has already been made. Pacing each day is extremely important and going to work on the A.B.E. chart will give you comfort and security.

It is only human to have thoughts about doing things and not quite getting around to doing them. However, another day is soon gone. The opportunity that may be yours within the next week, month or maybe even a year can be handled much more effectively if this homework has been completed.

Preparation of the A.B.E. Chart for the printer:

The professional quality of your A.B.E. chart will increase tenfold if you invest the modest amount necessary to have it typeset. One page is maximum and that page should reflect the very best that is *you*. Start with your name, address, phone number, and include the area code. Do not make any reference to age, hair color, eyes, weight, marital status or other personal information.

The most important line on any A.B.E. chart is the single statement of what you want to do. This should be stated clearly and simply, introduced by the words "Career Objective." This statement tells what you want. It will not explain what you can offer. It may be necessary to prepare several different A.B.E. charts to specify individual objectives for various companies. However, much of the time you will find your stated career objective is appropriate for almost any position you are seeking. You see, completing the preliminary research and homework will help you to clarify what it is you want. In going directly to the organizations in which you are interested, you will become visual and verbal.

Following the statement of career objective, drop down and devote one paragraph to *ability,* one to *background* and one to *experience.* It is important to include specific examples of successful performance and the results, whenever possible. You may wish to include testimonials praising your work and evidence of personal qualities which make it a pleasure to work with you. For example: The fund raiser you chaired for three consecutive years. You need not credit the committee chairman on your A.B.E. You were their leader; you put in the necessary time and motivation to realize the success. Now condense the report to dollars and cents realized because of your chairmanship. The business world listens with rapt attention when money speaks. I encourage you to become alert to the vocabulary that is effective in the competitive job market. The bottom line is performance.

The resume tradition has been to specify dates prominently out in the left margin or in a headline over each paragraph to command attention. *For you, the quality of your recent experience—what you have done—is far more important than the dates.* Put dates in their proper perspective and emphasize what you have accomplished during those years. Once again, let me caution you never to be discouraged or intimidated by a form that represents another's inability to keep up with the times. The forms that are floating around employment agencies are often so outdated that they do not deserve your time and talent. Prepare your personal A.B.E. chart and attach it to any form handed you.

Once again, for a thoroughly professional look, take your prepared chart to a typesetter. Keep your paragraphs short and your margins wide. Double space between paragraphs. It is permissible to center headlines and underline to stress accomplishments you most want employers to see. Take your typeset original to an offset printer and have a hundred copies prepared. Keep the original for additional copies if needed. Draw up a list of companies you will visit in person. Do not be tempted to hide behind direct mail or the telephone. Nothing succeeds like one's own personal introduction. Become verbal and visual and you will learn more in one day than you would learn in a month of waiting for the mail to arrive with answers.

Congratulations! You have come a long way. From starting to read about the plan for personal and professional growth, a slow and constant process has been evolving. The 3-S notebook should contain a good number of valid contacts. The practice in concentrated listening has surely proven helpful. Continue to seek out three persons each day in your quest for effective communication. I am hopeful the color-coded index card system is providing the discipline to assure progress on a number of important things. At this moment the index cards are ideal for putting a plan of monthly calls into action. Check the cards each morning to see your plan for the day.

Finally, the A.B.E. chart serves as a visual aid to tell the potential employer the many things that you have been doing in the past years. You will appreciate having invested the effort in preparing this chart.

Realities of Career Change

This chapter is directed to those who are employed now but want to change careers. So much thought goes into the possibility of changing jobs and so much wasted time is involved in only thinking. Great visions of the ideal position seem to occupy much of the imagination. The realities of the job search involve much more than daydreaming. For those who land the perfect job, there is usually a well-planned program involved. The most qualified person is often not the individual who gets the ideal job. Become the capable applicant and you will sweep aside your competition.

Endless hours of study spent attaining a degree, or a series of them, are too often dismissed by the interviewer. Employers are often amateurs when it comes to matching the most qualified applicants to the positions they have available. Does it seem wise to depend on employers to determine whether you are or are not qualified? Who knows what you can do better than you do? The person interviewing you is making an immediate judgment when you walk into the room, and the manner in which you present yourself and control the situation will determine how you are remembered. To articulate your greatest strengths, it is essential to be aware of your best capabilities. I want you to think of the conversation with the employer, or the individual who is interviewing you, as a message you have put in the form of a telegram, not a thesis. Think of how you would prepare a telegram. Select your words carefully and condense your message into a few sentences. Every word has meaning and the superfluous is dismissed. Keep this in mind during the brief time you have to showcase your qualifications and make a good impression.

Refer to the chapter which outlines the A.B.E. chart or professional resume. The one statement, after your name, address and phone contact, is your career objective. That statement should focus you clearly toward your goal. If you are uncertain about the direction you want to go, it may be important to obtain counseling before you attempt a career change. Properly analyzing one's own abilities is not easy, or even possible for some. Too many people aim themselves in the wrong direction with their first job and compound the error by building careers on the initial mistake. This lifelong entrapment is the result of allowing the heavy hand of fate to corrode the whole course of your future.

Career counseling: An excellent source of practical information is in Richard Nelson Bolles', *What Color Is Your Parachute?* You will find this paperback job manual available in almost every bookstore. The critical guides for choosing a professional career counselor are worth repeating here. Consider carefully the sound advice he gives. He suggests that *before* you choose a professional career counselor, you read these warnings three times.

1. Try to do these three steps toward a successful job hunt. Decide what you want to do. Decide where you want to do it. Then, thoroughly research the organizations in which you believe you are interested. Note: Seek out the person in each organization who has the power to hire you. Do not waste effort and energy talking with those who cannot make that decision.

2. Check with the library for books that may help you.

3. Should you decide you want professional help, choose at least three places to check out personally. Compare each of them and use good judgment.

4. Before visiting any of the agencies or consultants, you may find it valuable to spend some time at your library and research articles which will provide you with accurate guidelines to follow when you are speaking to any professional counselor.

In conclusion, I caution you not to sign any contracts unless you are convinced the promises are valid and the company will deliver everything you've discussed and the agreement so states. You may wish to take the contract to your lawyer before signing since the cost is usually high. It is far better to check it out prior to your decision than to wish you had done so later.

I felt it important to discuss the subject of professional counseling; however, I firmly believe that you have every skill and ability necessary to locate the ideal position for yourself. The money you save can be better spent on a glorious holiday. If you are serious about a job change, remember, be *visual* and *verbal.*

Two small words Starting with V. Take them seriously and you will have a third V, the award of Victory. Never will a contract be offered without your making a contact. The contact is speeded up and given a greater chance of success if you use the greatest selling power in the world—the act of being visual and of being verbal, in person. Mailing resumes and making countless phone calls is only wishful thinking, and filled with frustration and futility. Ask yourself the priceless question that often provides the motivation for action, "Just what is the worst thing that can happen if I go directly to the person who can open the door to that special job I want so much?" Answer that and you are on your way to becoming visual and verbal.

There are a few things I would suggest you avoid in your consideration of a job change. The very first rule is never to leave a present job until you have another position secured. The confidence you will feel and the power of negotiation is stronger with the knowledge that you have income and a place to return. The status of being unemployed puts an added strain on the applicant.

Avoid employment agencies, classified ads, research firms, and any promises of instant job choice. Nothing is instant and the fifteen percent of all jobs filled by the above means is a gamble at best. Those having tried the numbers game and allowed themselves the frustration of promised phone calls and the false hope of leads which never materialize, feel dejection and lose confidence in themselves. The idea of changing jobs is then put on the back burner and simmers another year or longer.

Also, avoid believing the statistics that the press pushes on us about unemployment, the rough going college graduates are going to have, the teaching field being glutted, the demand for engineers and scientists hitting a ten-year low. The words of doom go on and on and touch upon almost every industry. Don't believe everything you hear. There are vacancies and there is an ideal job for you. The difference between the negative and the positive is your attitude and your confidence in knowing you can uncover the work you will enjoy and work that will make the very most of your experience, skills, and assets.

I want to share a personal incident that allowed me the opportunity of helping a young woman uncover a job she had been seeking for six months. If you will bear with me, I'll take you from the beginning when I first spoke with her on the phone and how our conversation proved exceptionally productive for both of us.

My teenage daughter, Dana, and I were preparing to fly East and take the things she would be needing for her freshman year at Syracuse University. Because the size of Dana's trunk and suitcases would require a station wagon at the Syracuse airport, I called a car rental agency and spoke with an articulate and very competent young woman whose name was Cindy. She immediately handled the details of my special request and then took the extra step that makes the difference between just getting a job done and doing an exceptional job.

That step is "personalizing the transaction" and it involved the genuine interest Cindy showed when I mentioned Syracuse University. I shared the exciting news that our elder daughter was just starting her first experience of an East Coast college and of being on her own some three thousand miles from home. Cindy related to this because she had been out of college a short while and working for the car reservation department for just six months.

When I asked how she enjoyed the job, she confessed

it was O.K. She hesitated and then told me how very much she wanted to work for the airlines. In answer to my question about the number of interviews she had been on, I learned of one interview and the hope to have a second which would indicate a strong chance of being accepted. Cindy waited for the call and it did not come. She had built enormous hopes on the single call and felt personally rejected when she did not hear anything. Her next statements were a series of justifications about why she did not continue pursuing her search for an airline job. She talked about everything from the over-supply to the cutback in personnel and her frustration at hearing recorded messages by some of the airlines who were not hiring. My many years in the travel industry have shown me that people still are hired, and those who display determination and perserverance over-come the obstacles and get the jobs. They practice being visual and verbal.

When I asked Cindy if she believed every employee had been hired on their first interview, she thought a moment and said, "No, I guess not." By the time we completed our conversation, I was delighted to hear the spark of enthusiasm in her voice that told me she was primed to start again, and this time she would pursue and succeed.

Cindy was opening a door of opportunity for herself when she showed a sincere interest in another person. Her concern about my request for a larger car and the reason led our conversation into the area of her interest. Listening and caring move an ordinary conversation to a new level of meaning and everyone benefits. Practice this art at all times and a bonus of inner confidence and joy will be yours. Anytime you are visual and verbal you also have allowed yourself to become more vulnerable. By keeping yourself hidden behind the desk, phone, typewriter, and your tight circle of close acquaintances, you do not allow the world to reach you. Start an aggressive plan of action to break out of the old habits, listening to the same negative reports about the job market, and putting yourself down. Come to a screeching halt with all of that and anything else negative.

Where to Start: Take one full day to recharge and to redo yourself with a facial, massage, pedicure, manicure, and the very best haircut you can buy. Experiment with an updated hairstyle for that brand new you who is about to crash out of the old you. Try a makeup that adds more color and emphasizes the eyes, especially. Shop for the perfect interview image. The clothing should be of good quality. Don't skimp on price. Follow the complete look with the right shoes and a handsome attache case that will serve as your handbag and working briefcase.

Next Step: Review the Simplify-Satisfy chapter and remove any excess to clear the space for moving in an uninterrupted rhythm. This statement will not have meaning until you rid your home of the clutter that may have been building for a long time. The results of your decision to clean, condense and clear will be felt each day and carry over to the office.

Next Step: Prepare an Ability, Background and Experience chart. Have a hundred printed and keep some at your office and some at the Think Center in your home.

Next Step: The motivational tool of color-coded index cards can be a friend to you. Add a number of professional organizations that you plan to contact and attend their meetings. Jot information about them on one of the cards and note the follow-up on the consecutive card for the next week. Keep a running account of the groups you visit and of those you join. It is not necessary to join all of them, just the ones you realize can be beneficial to you in your plan of action. Networking is essential and you will find new associations helpful and enjoyable. Think of every individual you meet in an organization as contributing to part of a pyramid. Visualize the pyramids you may have visited in Egypt. If that trip is still in the future for you, visualize photographs of the pyramids. Here is how the pyramid system works. Start your conversation with the questions that indicate an interest in the work of the person to whom you are speaking. Follow the conversation with more specific questions, i.e. "Would you know about any departments hiring at this time? Tell me if you know of a certain need that the company has or a problem they seem to be troubled with recently." Keep the conversation flowing by sharing things you are doing at your job and how you are interested in a change of career and would appreciate any suggestions of people they know who are hiring. Do not put them on guard by asking for employment; just ask for names of people you might approach.

Each person's suggestion leads to others whom you can call or visit directly. Your conversation will include using the name of the person who had given you their name. That person may not have anything at the moment; but, if pressed for more contacts, they often give names that propel you to more leads and again you will start off the introduction by using the name of the person with whom you just spoke. Here is an excellent clue: Salespeople who call on companies are ideal sources of information about possible new positions and future openings. Get to know many men and women in sales and start the conversation flowing in a way that will allow you many leads to follow. Isn't the difference between motivation and procrastination very often a name of someone you can call? Putting off the search is done over and over because there are just no contacts. *It takes contacts to make contracts.*

The terrific jobs out there waiting for you depend on your willingness to be visual and verbal. Keep that 3-S (simple, small, spiral) notebook working for you. Be alert and really listen to three people each day. Those three may be the very contacts you need to open the door that has remained closed too long. Don't deny yourself another day—instead of wishing, start the doing. The future looks fantastic!

Interview - Rehearsed

You may be interested in the advice I give high school seniors at career day programs. First I appeal to them to continue their education while exploring directions until they find out what they really want to do. After a few examples and guidelines that work well for the age group, I ask for questions from the students. When they learn I have had a long association with the airlines, the questions break forth, and always with a similar theme. Repeatedly, they sound like this: "I would love to travel . . . how can I get a job with an airline? How much does it pay? Do you get a lot of passes right away? Oh, all those great places to go." They continue in that same glow of "me" goals. That is when I turn the interview over to them. I ask one of them to direct questions to me about why I want to work for the airline. My answer parrots the things I have just hear them say, with a slightly more tonal quality to highlight the selfishness that an employer would hear. The role playing takes less than ten minutes and the results are memorable. There is a stunned silence for a moment and then usually someone will raise her hand and ask if I would tell them the right things to say.

The same suggestions apply here. Mentally reverse an interview in your mind and practice how you can talk about your skills in a way that would obviously benefit the company. Remove the "I want" and the "me" thinking . . . it will only stand in the way of job opportunities. The manner in which you conduct yourself in an interview situation weighs critically on the decision-making process. There are many books, articles, cassettes, seminars, and workshops that offer training in the various methods to make you feel comfortable about an interview. However, many times the interview pops up unexpectedly and you take a deep breath and hope things will go well. The chances are slim that they will because an effective interview takes practice, research, study, and a distinct desire for the particular job.

I have learned through years of addressing groups, conducting workshops and talking privately with clients, people all seem to need more time. There does not seem to be enough time to read the books they really mean to read or to start the self-improvement programs they have in mind. I have said several times that I respect your time, and my writings reflect this in presenting solutions with a minimum amount of time spent dwelling on the problems. In practicing for an effective interview, the problem would seem to be one of the time it might take. Not so! The assignments given early in the book hopefully have become productive habits for you. The skill of listening attentively and the ability to communicate effectively will serve you well in any situation, and especially during an important interview.

Tape Recorders: Do you listen to cassettes? If you don't have a tape recorder, make yourself a gift of one at the earliest opportunity. The benefits are enormous! For example, anytime I am driving alone, I slip a cassette into the machine and have one of several motivational speakers to keep me company. Cavett Robert, Zig Ziglar, Og Mandino, Dr. Norman Vincent Peale, and many others are excellent and provide ideas and inspiration. I take the recorder on some of my speaking assignments and tape myself. This gives me the opportunity to review my speech on the way home. Continual improvement is top priority to a speaker and only by listening to yourself and to audience response can you evaluate how to improve your presentation. Here is another way I find tapes exceptionally helpful. I am continually training instructors whom I have interviewed and found qualified to teach my personalized time management course. However, since they necessarily are located some distance from each other, it is inconvenient for them to meet as a group in my office for the two-day training. So, I send my personal instruction to them on tapes and support it with an instruction book. They send a tape back to me with questions and I reply on tape. We have developed a training process that is an improvement over letters and much less expensive than long distance phone calls. The convenience of speaking on tape can be of great benefit to anyone eager to save time. Talking is easier than typing and surely faster than handwriting. You'll find many uses for it. As soon as you have the recorder, do begin to practice for interviews.

In the beginning, turn the recorder on while you are talking to your family, perhaps during the dinner hour. Turn the tape on "record" the next time you are chatting on the phone or when a neighbor drops by. This is for a purpose. You will be able to hear yourself as others do. If this is the first time you have heard yourself on tape, be prepared to not recognize the voice as yours. After the initial shock, listen for intonation, pitch, cliches, and exaggerated superlatives such as marvelous! . . . or divine! . . . or fantastic! Notice your inflections. When you raise your voice at the end of the word "really", it suggests surprise. Drop the voice on the second syllable and the message is different.

Pretend you are standing in front of a group of runners and it is up to you to say, "Ready, get set, go!" Say it out loud and notice how you say "ready." Your voice does not raise and signify a question; it stays firm and is a command. When someone uses a rising inflection, it can indicate uncertainty. This is often a way of asking permission from the listener.

Listen to your tapes some more and see if you are using the words "I guess" or "I suppose." Your conversations should consist of positive statements. Avoid the tendency to modify your opinions. Say what you feel and try not to sound uncommitted. Earlier I mentioned using the word "just" to qualify any label you might use to describe yourself. Never do this, because it transmits a sense of insecurity. Other words you may hear over and over on the tape are "really" and "so." Your goal is to learn to speak in a professional manner. Although there are many methods available to teach you this skill, they will cost a great deal and take time you may not have to spare. So, with the recorder try to listen to yourself each day. I recommend the same place and the same time because it will help establish the project.

After a few weeks of hearing yourself each day on the tape, ask a friend to role play an actual interview situation with you. Ideally, someone with personnel experience or an employer who does interviewing regularly would be the one to ask. However, that may not be possible and, assuming that it is not, we will take a list of the most asked questions and practice.

A natural opener is, *"Tell me a little about yourself."* You may want to toss a question back and ask what he or she would like to know; however, this is not a good idea. Be prepared to make a summary statement about yourself. You may want to include your skills, your interests, and the reason you are seeking a position with that particular firm. Keep the answer brief so you can move the conversation toward questions about the job. Your purpose for coming is to learn more about the position. The interviewer is facing the task of filling the position and wants to be sold on your qualifications so the job can be filled and he or she can move on to another task. Every career counselor and many books on the topic will strongly advise you to be well-prepared before you go for the interview. Find out as much as you can about the company, industry, organization and, if possible, the person to whom you will be speaking. A current annual report on the company is an excellent source of background information. Libraries may carry them if it is a large firm. If you are applying for a position with a small business, it may be possible to talk with one of the employees before your interview and the information could prove helpful. There may be a time when you cannot do research or ask anyone, but it's a rare employer who isn't proud to share information if the questions are asked with tact and respect. "Do you mind if I ask a question?" or "With regard to that, could you tell me . . . ?" Keep in mind how your skills can help with the problems of the company.

"Why do you want to work for this company?" Have an answer ready that includes mention of your strengths and what you can offer the firm.

"Are you planning to have a family?" This question is now illegal so you may: (1) Tell the interviewer it is illegal; (2) Tell the interviewer it is a personal question and you would rather not answer; (3) Explain you are

interested in hearing more about the job and, for now, you are planning a career.

"I see you have three children, Mrs. Jones. How will you be able to work?" Again your answer can point out it is an illegal question; however, it may be easier to say simply that their care has been arranged and that you feel you can be on the job during the hours expected. It is important not to feel you must justify your children. That is too ridiculous. The subject really should not be mentioned since it is rarely brought up during any male interview.

"If we offer this job to you, what is the least amount of money you would consider?" Watch this as a loaded question and turn it back to the interviewer. Ask, "Are you offering me this position?" Do not start any negotiation of salary before receiving the offer to work. Pull answers from the interviewer by asking questions. Here is a response you might want to use. "I would not expect an amount of money out of proportion to the responsibility, but I believe it should be competitive with your salaries for similar positions. Tell me the amount you had in mind."

If still pressed for a figure, never give one specific amount. Draw a range, for example, $18,000 to $22,000.

The questions you could be asked are unlimited. They will start with the request to explain the hows, whys, whens, wheres, whos, and whats. When any open-ended question is asked, you can respond with at least a sentence. Keep the interview moving back and forth with equal questions from you. Do not simply answer the questions because then you have no control of the conversation or of the interview. Show your skills by turning this opportunity into a selling situation. Speak in a manner that dictates professionalism and be genuinely interested in learning how you can help solve problems.

You will want to role play some of the initial steps which precede sitting down to talk. The manner in which you walk into the office is of prime importance because the first impression can be crucial. Arrive well ahead of the appointed time and sit quietly to collect and calm yourself. Introduce yourself to the receptionist, secretary, or whomever it is you meet first. If you are asked to wait, take a seat and review some of the things you may have learned about the company. You will have your A.B.E. chart ready to leave with the person in charge. If requested to fill out any forms, attach it to the application.

Your confidence in yourself will be assured if you have taken care in your grooming and clothing selection. Avoid any tendency to straighten your scarf or blouse or other gestures which are signs of nervousness. Body language plays a large part in the poise and confidence you want to portray. It will help to rehearse all of this in front of a mirror before you take on a live audience. This may seem like too much effort but it will serve you well on the day you need it most. Spend a few minutes each day for a couple of weeks practicing in front of a large mirror and take the same time to rehearse your answers to some of the questions you can be sure will be asked. Turn the cassette recorder on and you will have an audio-video tape working for you. The mirror will reflect how you appear to others and hearing the voice repeated back will allow you to make improvements.

When the time for your appointment arrives and you are shown into the room, walk directly over to the person and extend your hand for a firm handshake. Smile and exchange the usual pleasantries about the weather or make a comment about a painting, a photo or something else of obvious interest to the interviewer. Where the interviewer sits establishes a mood. If it is behind a desk and in a slightly higher chair, that will denote power and give the interviewer psychological control over the situation. The informal situation might include a sofa and chair, two chairs, or two sofas. If you find there is no chair immediately by the desk do not hesitate to ask if you might move one closer. Occasionally, such situations are purposely arranged to witness what an applicant will do. Be assertive to the point of treating yourself with respect. Expecting the best will often result in receiving it. As the interview starts, try not to appear distracted or look at your watch, and avoid any appearance of being in a hurry. It is best not to smoke and, of course, do not chew gum. Many things will come spontaneously, and they should. The secret is to be natural and let the enthusiasm and eagerness about the potential position really come through to the interviewer. Affecting too cool and collected an attitude can ruin the chance of being hired. You know the feeling that a lack of response can give when you are speaking to someone. Silence is sometimes interpreted as hostility and invites rejection. The most important thing is to participate in the interview with the self-approving conviction that you are you.

In summary, the practice will give you the poise to feel like a winner and not a victim. A friend who has been in personnel for many years explained the one common mistake many applicants make is just failing to believe in themselves. They really are the victim. Before any change can occur, the attitude must become positive. This brings us full circle and back to the positive thinking I introduced in the first chapter. Know who you are and like who it is you are. If you are sure of your direction, know your objective and show a sincere interest in a way of bringing the very best of yourself to the surface . . . the result is certain to be one of success. Not every interview is going to mean you land the job you want; however, it prepares you for the next and the next and you continue learning and knowing you are moving straight ahead to the place you want to be.

Quick Wrap-Up

Looking for the most condensed, concise, and briefest explanation possible? You are my kind of person! This "wrap-up" is for you. I really mean it.

This book developed because women came up to me following my seminars and workshops and told me they wanted to start planning for a career but didn't know what they could do or where to start. I heard myself giving the same advice so often that the need for a book became obvious.

My immediate response was to convince each of these women how individual and uniquely special they were in their interests and skills. Next, I encouraged them to practice Dale Carnegie's six basic rules:

1. Become genuinely interested in other people.

2. Smile

3. Remember another's name.

4. Be a good listener.

5. Ask about the interests of another person.

6. Make other people feel important and do it sincerely.

This method of communication can open countless doors which would otherwise remain firmly closed until the warmth of genuine caring opens them.

My next suggestion was to keep a small spiral notebook with them at all times and start the habit of collecting contacts. The contacts one makes today become contracts tomorrow and this rule applies to any business, any position, and any organization. A practice of truly listening will result in warmer and more important friendships.

An individual's self-image is closely related to outer appearance. For anyone who does not feel completely confident in the results of their own efforts, I suggest a professional consultant to help achieve the look that is essential in today's highly competitive job market. This investment of time and money pays large dividends and should be considered by anyone serious about a career and doubting their own ability to select the right wardrobe.

An individual can progress smoothly when the stop and start of daily routine is changed to an even rhythm of pacing the day. Review how to create this system and establish a simplified method of managing and maintaining the home.

The key to accomplishment is the motivation one feels to do the things necessary for success. My simplified method of personal motivation consists of a notebook ring and color-coded index cards. Because of the simplicity, the chances of it working are greatly increased. Complex systems are doomed to failure and, in contrast, you will find this method is easy and fun. Most importantly . . . it motivates!

You may feel any career choice for you is a distant dream. Perhaps young children or a full schedule of classes are now the priority that demands all of your time and energy. Knowing what half-steps can mean in your life is vital to your future. A small portion of each day spent taking half-steps will provide the confidence and skills you need in preparation for the time when you will be ready to take the full step. Turn back to the chapter on half-steps and read about the life experiences of several young women whom I describe. This may serve as the stimulus you need to get started on a regular half-step pattern in your life. It is *never* too early. I really mean it when I say that the most direct path to success in finding the career you want is by learning to be *visual* and *verbal.* To persist is to achieve, and with a list of personal contacts (gathered over a period of time in your 3-S notebook) you can go in person to seek the opportunities for the right career. You will take with you the life experience chart to serve as your professional resume. You will have rehearsed the job interview and feel prepared and poised.

Be selective in your quest . . . continue the search . . . and the results will be worth your effort.

Bibliography

Berman, Eleanor. *Re-Entering: Successful Back to Work Strategies for Women Seeking a Fresh Start.* New York: Crown Publishers, Inc., 1980.

Bird, Caroline. *The Two Paycheck Marriage.* New York: Pocket Books, 1970.

Bolles, Richard Nelson. *What Color Is Your Parachute? Practical Manual for Job-Hunters and Career-Changers.* Berkeley, California: Ten Speed Press, 1977.

Boros, James M. & Parkinson, Robert Dr. J. *How To Get A Fast Start in Today's Job Market.* Englewood Cliffs, New Jersey: Prentice-Hall, 1980.

Bostwick, Burdette E. *Finding the Job You've Always Wanted.* New York: John Wiley and Sons, 1977.

Cardozo, Arlene Rossen. *Woman At Home.* New York: Doubleday, 1976.

Carnegie, Dale. *How to Enjoy Your Life and Your Job.* New York: Pocket Books, 1970.

Curtis, Jean. *A Guide For Working Mothers.* New York: Doubleday and Company, Inc., 1975.

Dusay, John M. M.D. *Egograms.* New York: Harper & Row, 1977.

Evatt, Crislynne. *How To Organize Your Closet . . . and your life!* San Francisco: Entheos, 1980.

Fader, Shirley Sloan. *From Kitchen to Career.* New York: Stein and Day, 1977.

Fensterheim, Herbert Ph.D. and Baer, Jean. *Don't Say Yes When You Want To Say No.* New York: Dell Publishing Co. Inc., 1975.

Gray, Eileen. *Everywoman's Guide to College.* Millbrae, California: Les Femmes, 1975.

Harding, Esther M. *The Way Of All Women.* New York: Harper Colophon Books, Harper & Row, 1975.

Hauser, Gayelord. *Be Happier, Be Healthier.* Greenwich, Connecticut: Fawcett Publications, Inc., 1960.

Heim, Jane A. *Directory of Working Women. Resource Guide for Women Returning to Work.* Naperville, Illinois: Jane Heim and Associates, 1980.

Hemingway, Patricia Drake. *The Well Dressed Woman. A Complete Guide to Creating the Right Look for Yourself and Your Career.* New York: David McKay Company, Inc., 1977.

James, Muriel and Jongeward, Dorothy. *Born To Win: Transactional Analysis with Gestalt Experiments.* Reading, Massachusetts: Addison-Wesley Publishing Company, 1975.

Keane, Betty Winkler. *Sensing: Letting Yourself Live. Book and Cassette.* New York: Harper and Row, 1979.

Lair, Jacqueline Carey and Lair, Jess Ph.D. *"Hey God, What Should I Do Now?"* New York: Fawcett-Crest Books, 1973.

Lathrop, Richard. *Who's Hiring Who.* Reston, Virginia: Reston Publishing Company, Inc. A Prentice-Hall Company, 1976.

Mademoiselle. *Success: College and Job.* New York: Conde Nast Publications, Inc., August, 1980.

Nash, Katherine. *Get the Best of Yourself: How to Discover Your Success Pattern and Make It Work for You.* New York: Grosset & Dunlap, Inc., 1976.

Ortlund, Anne. *Disciplines of the Beautiful Woman.* Waco, Texas: Word, Incorporated, 1977.

Peale, Norman Vincent Dr. *The Power of Positive Thinking.* New York: Fawcett-Crest Books, 1952.

Peale, Norman Vincent Dr. *Creative Help for Daily Living.* New York: Foundation for Christian Living, 1980.

Pollack, Ted, Ph.D. *Managing Yourself Creatively*, New York: Hawthorn Books, Inc., 1971.

Rosenthal, Ed & Lichty, Ron. *132 Ways to Earn a Living (Without Working for Someone Else)*. New York: St. Martin's Press.

Schwartz, Felice N., Schifter Margaret H., Gillotti, Susan S. *How to Go to Work When Your Husband Is Against It, Your Children Aren't Old Enough, and There's Nothing You Can Do Anyhow*. New York: Simon & Schuster, 1972.

Seaman, Florence Dr. and Orimer, Anne. *Winning At Work. A Book for Women.* Philadelphia, Pennsylvania: Running Press, 1979.

Stone, Janet and Bachner, Jane. *Speaking Up A Book for Every Woman Who Wants to Speak Effectively.* New York: McGraw-Hill, 1977.

Towle, Charlotte. *Common Human Needs.* New York: National Association of Social Workers, Inc., 1965.

Trahey, Jane. *Jane Trahey on Women and Power.* New York: Avon Books, 1977.

Ullmann, Liv. *Changing.* New York: Bantam Books, Inc., 1978.

Walters, Dottie. *Never Underestimate The Selling Power Of A Woman.* New York: Frederick Fell Publishers, Inc., 1978.

Wetherby, Terry. *Conversations. Working Women talk about doing a "man's job".* Millbrae, California: Les Femmes, 1977.

Working Woman Magazine. *New Career Guide.* New York: Hal Publications, September, 1979.

You may want the convenience of a Simplified Career Guide workbook. This slim booklet contains a sample A.B.E. Chart, a checklist of professional preparation for the applicant, a recap of interview techniques and special emphasis on clues toward motivation.

A coupon has been provided for your convenience. Copies of Everywoman's Guide to Time Management and the convenient Household Information Manual in which to record the pertinent data which personalizes the needs of you and your family can also be ordered.

For those of you interested in Travel, you will find Everywoman's Guide to Travel provides basic and practical information.

Simplified Career Guide

Send order to:
ESTE ASSOCIATES Suite #443
Wharfside Bldg., 680 Beach Street
San Francisco, California 94109

Make check payable to:
ESTE ASSOCIATES

Simplified Career
   Guide $2.00
Household Information
   Manual $2.00
Everywoman's Guide to
   Time Management. . $5.00
Everywoman's Guide
   To Travel $5.00

NAME _____

STREET_____

CITY _____

STATE _____ZIP _____

For additional information about cassettes, programs and the instructor program, phone the ESTE offices 415/441-4312

SHIPPING & HANDLING CHART

All postage, shipping and handling charges are figured together in this easy to read chart. Use order form. INCLUDE shipping charge.

No Stamps or COD's Please. Send Check or Money Order

IF YOUR ORDER IS:

		UP to $3.00–Add 85¢
$3.01	to	$5.00–Add $1.15
$5.01	to	$7.00–Add $1.45
$7.01	to	$9.00–Add $1.65
$9.01	to	$11.00–Add $1.85
$11.01	to	$13.00–Add $2.05
$13.01	to	$15.00–Add $2.25
$15.01	to	$17.00–Add $2.50
Add 10¢ for each dollar over $17		